SAM STIER AND JEAN POTTER

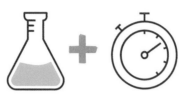

SCIENCE IN SECONDS FOR KIDS

100+ Activities You Can Do in Ten Minutes or Less

SECOND EDITION

JOSSEY-BASS™
A Wiley Brand

First edition copyright © 1995 by Jean Potter.
Published by Jossey-Bass
A Wiley Imprint
111 River St., Hoboken N.J. 07030
www.josseybass.com
Published simultaneously in Canada.

Jossey-Bass books and products are available through most bookstores. To contact Jossey-Bass directly call our Customer Care Department within the U.S. at 800-956-7739, outside the U.S. at 317-572-3986, or fax 317-572-4002.

Jossey-Bass also publishes its books in a variety of electronic formats. Some content that appears in print may not be available in electronic books.

Library of Congress Cataloging-in-Publication Data

Names: Stier, Sam, author. | Potter, Jean, 1947- author.
Title: Science in seconds for kids : over 100 experiments and activities
  you can do in ten minutes or less / Sam Stier, Jean Potter.
Description: Second edition. | Hoboken, N.J. : Jossey-Bass, [2021] |
  Includes index.
Identifiers: LCCN 2020027684 (print) | LCCN 2020027685 (ebook) | ISBN
  9781119685470 (paperback) | ISBN 9781119685500 (adobe pdf) | ISBN
  9781119685517 (epub)
Subjects: LCSH: Science—Experiments—Juvenile literature.
Classification: LCC Q164 .S78 2021 (print) | LCC Q164 (ebook) | DDC
  507.8—dc23
LC record available at https://lccn.loc.gov/2020027684
LC ebook record available at https://lccn.loc.gov/2020027685

Cover Design: Wiley
Cover Images: chemistry icon © M.Style/Shutterstock, timer © iconim/Shutterstock, kids style font © Knstart Studio/Shutterstock

SECOND EDITION SKY10021689_101320

This book is dedicated to my dear friend James H. Harless in appreciation for his friendship and love for fellow man and for his significant contributions to the field of education.

— **Jean**

To teachers everywhere who guide children toward a good life by fostering wonder, curiosity, and discovery – sensations evolution has given us the capacity to feel that have made humankind what it is today.

— **Sam**

Special thanks to:

Robert M. Frostig, science teacher, Horace Mann Junior High School, Charleston, West Virginia.

Michael J. Chovanec, physics teacher; Tobin George, biology teacher; William Fry, science teacher; Hempfield Area High School, Greensburg, Pennsylvania.

Additional thanks to:

Thomas, my husband, for his incredible love and support.
Archie, our Welsh Corgi, for his companionship and friendship.
Shadow, our Russian Blue, for his constant vigil.
Mary, my friend, for love, understanding, and support.
Mom, Dad, Kathy, and Emmett, my family, for so many reasons.
Kate Bradford, my editor, for her expert opinion and advice.

Sam Stier would like to thank his most capable agent, Grace Freedson, for helping create the opportunity to work on this book, and Jean Potter, for putting the wonderful first edition of this book together. The challenge of explaining a wide range of fascinating, complicated physical phenomena to young children has been a wonderful opportunity to try and explain a wide range of fascinating, complicated physical phenomena to myself.

Contents

Introduction

Science in Seconds for Kids contains 108 quick and easy activities and experiments that will help you discover the wonders of science and our world, from how rockets work to what causes lightning. Each activity takes only 10 minutes or less to complete. You will soon be able to look quickly into many exciting topics.

How This Book Is Organized

Science in Seconds for Kids is divided into sections by topic. If you are looking for a particular activity, you can find it in the Activities Index at the back of the book.

Each activity answers a particular question about science and includes a list of the materials you need, easy-to-follow steps, and an explanation of what the activity demonstrates. There is no need to buy special materials, but you may want to visit the Internet or a library for additional information on the topic.

Tips for Completing the Activities

Try to be very careful as you perform your activities. These tips will help:

Be prepared. Read through any activity before you begin to do it. Collect all the materials required before you start, and place them in the order in which you will use them. Science can be messy, so wear old clothes while doing activities. Give yourself enough space to work and enough ventilation. Cover surfaces with newspaper in case of spills.

Be accurate. When conducting your activities, follow the directions closely, and write down all results. Consider repeating experiments to see if you get the same result again. Doing an experiment more than once can help improve the accuracy of your results.

Be creative. After completing an activity according to the directions, try to think of ways that you can change an experiment. Look for the results from your change to the experiment. Before you make the change, ask an adult if your substitution is all right.

Be careful. Ask for adult assistance and supervision when using sharp instruments. Materials should be used for the purpose for which they are intended. Work cautiously.

Be neat. Keep your work and your work area as neat as you can. Use clean instruments, and wash them after every use. Put your materials away after they have been washed.

Have fun! Because our world is so interesting, science is full of discoveries and adventure that lasts forever!

Image by Free-Photos from Pixabay

Air

Air is a special mixture of gases that surrounds and protects our planet and makes Life possible. Since it is colorless, odorless, and tasteless, we sometimes do not remember it is there. But it is, and it is very important.

Air has many uses, from keeping living things alive to making it possible for you to play basketball, fly a kite, or fly in an airplane. In this section, you will do some activities and experiments to learn how air can push objects, lift things, and make balls bounce.

Dry Paper
Can Paper Stay Dry in Water?

Materials

tap water

plastic tub

sheet of paper

plastic cup

Try This

1. Run tap water into the plastic tub until the tub is about three-fourths full.

2. Crumple the sheet of paper and push it to the bottom of the plastic cup. Use enough paper so it will stay at the bottom when the cup is upside down.

3. Hold the cup upside down and push it into the water. Be sure to hold the cup straight up and down, not tilted.

4. Pull the cup straight up out of the water and, with dry hands, remove the paper. What happens to the paper?

What's Going On?

The paper did not get wet. Air surrounded the paper in the cup. When you pushed the cup into the water, the air was trapped in the cup. The trapped air pushed back on the water, keeping it from reaching the paper. If you had tilted the cup, the air would have escaped, and the water would have taken its place. In that case, the paper would have become wet.

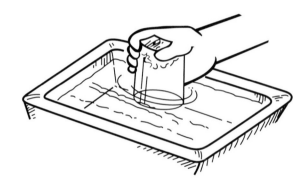

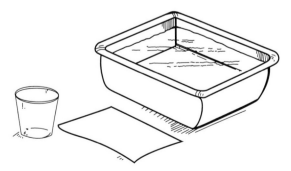

Elastic Air

Why Does a Balloon Filled with Air Bounce?

Materials

balloon

string

Try This

1. Inflate the balloon.

2. Tie the neck of the balloon closed. Tie a string to the neck.

3. With your hand, push in the balloon at different places.

4. Bounce the balloon against a table or your fist. What happens to the balloon when you press or bounce it against something?

What's Going On?

Balloons are made of an **elastic** (stretchy) material called **latex**. When you blew air into the balloon, the air **molecules** (the smallest particle or amount of a chemical substance) were packed closer and closer together. When you pushed in on the balloon, you actually felt all those air molecules pushing back. Because the balloon and air are elastic, the balloon bounced back when you pushed it against a table or your hand. If the balloon were filled with sand, it would not bounce! This is why basketballs, soccer balls, and other balls are filled with air.

Air Rocket
What Happens to Air When You Squeeze It?

Materials

piece of string about 6 ft (2 m) long

2 chairs

drinking straw

long balloon

masking tape

Try This

1. Tie one end of the piece of string to the first chair.

2. Lace the string through the drinking straw.

3. Tie the other end of the string to the second chair.

4. Move the chairs apart so the string is stretched tight.

5. Inflate the balloon and hold the neck so that no air escapes.

6. Keep the neck of the balloon closed as you tape the balloon to the straw.

7. When the balloon is taped, release the neck. What happens?

What's Going On?

The balloon was forced along the string. When you inflated the balloon, you pushed air into it, stretching out the latex skin. The elastic skin of the balloon then put **pressure**, or **force**, on the air inside the balloon. When you released the balloon, the air rushed out one end with a force that pushed the balloon in the opposite direction. When a rocket is launched, tremendous force is required to lift it off the ground. The rocket gets this force from fuel, which is **ignited** (set on fire), forcing heated gas out the end of the rocket, pushing the rocket up in the other direction.

Air Push
Air Pressure Is All Around Us

Materials

5-by-8-in. index card

plastic cup

tap water

bowl

Try This

1. Make sure the index card is large enough to completely cover the top of the plastic cup.

2. Fill the cup with tap water to the brim so that no air space remains.

3. Place the index card on top of the cup. Make sure there is no air between the card and the water. If there is air space, remove the card, add more water, and replace the card.

4. Hold the card in place by putting one hand on it.

5. Turn the cup upside down over the bowl and slowly remove your hand from under the card.

6. Turn the cup slowly in different directions. Can you make the card stay on the glass when you move it in different directions?

What's Going On?

The air that surrounds us pushes in all directions. When you turned the water-filled cup upside down, the air around the cup maintained its pressure on the index card and held it in place, even against the weight of the water. The card will stay pressed against the cup until a force stronger than the surrounding air moves it.

Air Support

How Does the Shape of an Object Affect How It Falls Through the Air?

Materials

scissors

ruler

8-foot (2.4-m) piece of string

2 square handkerchiefs

2 clothespins or small binder clip

Try This

1. Cut the piece of string into eight 1-foot (30-cm) lengths.

2. Tie a big knot in the middle of one handkerchief.

3. Tie one length of string to each corner of each handkerchief.

4. Gather the ends of the loose strings leading from each handkerchief and tie them in a knot around the head of each clothespin or similarly weighted object.

5. Grip the center of each handkerchief and toss both handkerchiefs into the air, or drop them from a high place. What happens?

What's Going On?

The handkerchief knotted in the middle fell to earth faster than the unknotted handkerchief. When an object falls through the air, it hits air molecules. Each molecule pushes up slightly on the falling object. Because the unknotted handkerchief was able to spread out, it caught more air molecules, which slowed its fall.

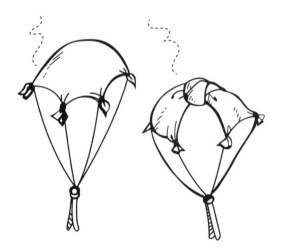

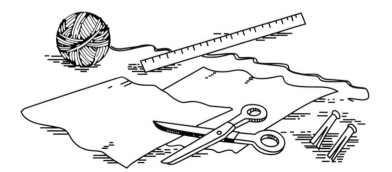

Bottle Balloon

What Happens to Air When It Is Heated and Cooled?

Materials

balloon

2-liter soda bottle

hot tap water

2 cake pans

ice tap water

adult helper

Try This

1. Fit the balloon over the mouth of the soda bottle.

2. Ask your adult helper to pour the hot water into the first cake pan.

3. Pour the ice water into the second pan.

4. Place the bottle with the balloon in the pan of hot water for a few seconds and observe what happens.

5. Remove the bottle from the hot water and place it in the ice water. What happens to the balloon this time?

What's Going On?

The bottle looked empty but was filled with air molecules. These molecules constantly moved around inside the bottle. The warmer the molecules, the more they move and the more room they occupy. When you put the bottle with the balloon over the hot water, the balloon **inflated**, or expanded with air, because the air molecules began moving around more and occupying more space. When you put the bottle with the balloon over the ice water, the balloon **deflated**, or collapsed, because the molecules moved closer together and occupied less space.

Book Lift
Can Air Lift Heavy Objects?

Materials

plastic shopping bag with no holes

book

Try This

1. Place the shopping bag on a table.
2. Place the book on the bag.
3. Arrange the bag so the open end extends off the table. The book should not extend off the table.
4. Lifting the bag a little, blow very hard into the open end. What happens to the book?

What's Going On?

When you blew into the bag, the book rose off the table. The extra air molecules you added to the bag pushed against each other, causing the bag to expand and lift the book. You blew air into the bag much the way you pump air into tires. Air is so strong that, inside tires, it can hold up cars or large trucks!

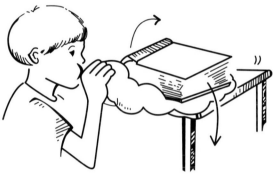

Lifting Things with No Hands
How Can Air Lift Planes?

Materials

Used, flexible dollar bill or similar-sized piece of paper.

Try This

1. Place the edge of the short end of a used, flexible dollar bill against your bottom lip.
2. Blow air straight forward out of your mouth in a constant, firm stream.
3. What happens to the dollar bill?

What's Going On?

When you blow, the air above the dollar bill starts to move and spread out. The air under the bill moves upward to fill up the extra space, much like a balloon expanding with greater air pressure as it is filled up. The result is that the dollar bill lifts, with no one pulling it up, as if by magic. This is the same reason why air can lift up and keep an entire jet airplane in the sky, just from air pushing upward on its wings from below as the plane moves forward.

Dusty Air

What Is in the Air?

Materials

flashlight

Try This

1. Turn on the flashlight.
2. Darken the room.
3. Direct the light beam on an object and look at the air space between the flashlight and the object. What do you see?

What's Going On?

When you looked at the flashlight beam, you saw tiny **particles** (very tiny pieces) floating through the air. The Earth's air is not just pure gas. It also contains particles of dirt, sand, cloth, metal, wood, plastic, ash, hair, and other materials. When the air becomes full of manufactured particles, such as soot, ash, or chemicals, we say it is **polluted**. Polluted air can be harmful to people and pets. That's one reason why spending time outdoors, opening windows, and having lots of indoor plants is good for people.

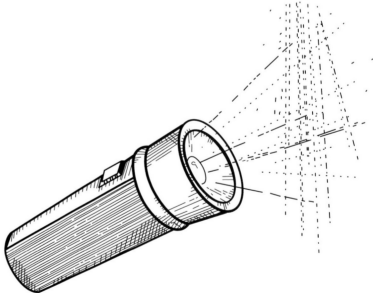

Image by joakant from Pixabay

Living Things

We're lucky to live on a fascinating planet full of extraordinary forms of Life. Some creatures are huge – larger than school buses — while some cannot be seen without the aid of a microscope. Regardless of the form of Life, each one is fascinating to learn about.

In this section, you will discover many things about living things. You will find out how earthworms stay clean even while sliding through the mud. You will learn why eggs are round. And you will discover the different reasons why trees don't break even when the wind blows hard.

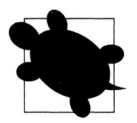

Whopping Hoppers
How Far Can Grasshoppers Hop?

Materials

tape measure

colorful object

Try This

1. Go outside and try to find a cricket, grasshopper, or other hopping creature. Observe how it moves.

2. Ask for help measuring your height.

3. Using a colorful object, mark out a distance on the floor or ground that is 20 times your height (this means adding your height to itself 20 times).

4. Try making one big leap toward the colorful object. How close did you get?

What's Going On?

Many common animals can do uncommonly amazing things. Grasshoppers, for example, can hop about 20 times the length of their bodies. If you could do what grasshoppers do every day, you could hop the distance you just marked out on the ground in a single leap!

Smart Skin

How Do Earthworms Stay So Clean?

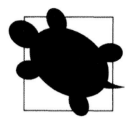

Materials

long, skinny balloon

sink

Try This

1. Blow up the balloon and tie it off.

2. Turn on a pencil-thin stream of water in the sink.

3. Move the side of the balloon up next to the stream of water, without touching it. Does the stream of water do anything?

4. Now rub the balloon vigorously on your hair.

5. Once again, move the side of the balloon up next to the stream of water, without touching it. What happens to the stream of water?

What's Going On?

By rubbing the balloon on your head, you added a bunch of small particles to it (called "electrons") from your hair, which gave the balloon a negative charge, making it act temporarily almost like a magnet. Water molecules are attracted to these small particles, so the stream of water now bends toward the balloon. This is the same way that earthworms never take a bath but manage to stay so clean, even while they crawl through the dirt all day. When an earthworm starts moving, friction makes electrons from the soil collect on the worm's skin. Water in the soil is then attracted toward the earthworm, cleaning the worm as it travels, and also making the earthworm's journey through the soil more slippery and easier.

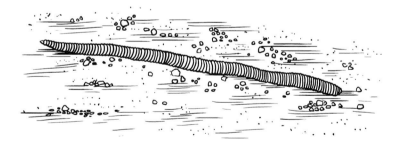

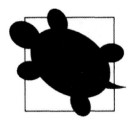

Break an Egg

Why Can't You Break an Egg by Squeezing?

Materials

raw egg

sink

frying pan or bowl

Try This

1. Over the sink, place a raw egg in your palm, wrap your fingers around it (no rings), and squeeze as hard as you can. Can you break it?

2. Now hit the egg over the edge of a frying pan or bowl.

3. Examine the shell bits of the egg. Try to crack one of the bigger fragments with your fingers. Is it very thick? Is it very strong?

What's Going On?

Eggs are designed to be both strong and weak. An egg is constructed to support the weight of a mother bird sitting on it (incubating the young bird within). Egg shell material is very thin, brittle, and doesn't weigh much. Instead, the egg gets its strength from its **shape**. The shape of the egg spreads and transfers the weight of the mother bird all around the egg. Her weight is supported by the entire egg. When you hit the egg on the edge of the frying pan, all the force is concentrated on a small part of the eggshell. Likewise, a baby bird can peck the shell from within using its pointed beak, and the egg will break to let it out.

Egg Shape

Why Aren't Eggs Perfectly Round?

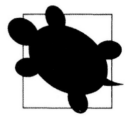

Materials

egg (hard-boiled or not)

round ball

Try This

1. Place the egg and the ball on the floor.
2. Roll each one. Which one rolls more easily?

What's Going On?

When you rolled the ball, it moved easily across the floor. The egg rolled a little, but mostly it just wobbled. Which shape would more easily roll out of a bird's nest?

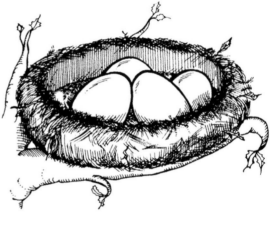

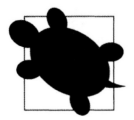

Seeing Without Eyes
Can You See with Your Fingertips?

Materials

a long, clean, adult-sized sock

several natural objects, such as a shell, pinecone, feather

Try This

1. Ask an adult to put one of the natural objects deep inside the sock.

2. Reach inside the sock and explore the object with your fingers. Pay attention to the details of its shape and texture.

3. Did you notice things about the object that you hadn't realized before?

4. Repeat with the other natural objects.

What's Going On?

Everything in the natural world is full of design. The way each thing is designed helps it work. Shape, texture, color, strength — all of these things can be important.

When we recognize what something is, like a feather, we often stop looking further at it. By removing the use of your eyes, you explored each object in a new way, and "saw" them again as though for the very first time. This allowed you to discover new things about these familiar items, even better than if you used your eyes.

Bendy Trees

How Do Tree Rings Help Trees Not Break?

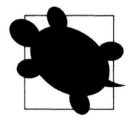

Materials

a piece of wood with exposed tree rings

a paperback book

a hand lens (optional)

Try This

1. Look at the rings in the piece of wood. Notice how dark-colored rings alternate with light-colored rings.

2. Hold the book parallel to the floor between your fingers, midway along the binding, letting the pages droop. Twist your wrist slowly to rotate the book. Notice how the pages adjust.

What's Going On?

Trees add material to their trunks in rings each year. Each pair of light and dark rings represents a year of growth. The light rings grow in the spring, when there is lots of water. The dark rings grow in the summer/fall, when there is less water. That's why the dark rings are narrower, since they grow slowly, and they have less spaces in the wood (which gives them a darker color), making this wood stiff. The lighter rings are wider, since they grow quickly, and they have more spaces in the wood (which give them a lighter color), making this wood more flexible. Like the twisting book, whose pages can slide past each other, the alternating stiff and flexible wood rings allow the trees to bend in the wind more easily, without breaking.

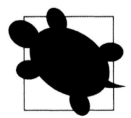

Tree Curves

Why Are Tree Trunks Curved at the Bottom?

Materials

a tree outdoors, the older the better

a clear, plastic (#1) container from the grocery store (e.g., for berries)

scissors

polarized sunglasses

cell phone or computer screen

Try This

1. Look at the biggest, oldest tree you can find. Notice how the trunk meets the ground. Does the base of the tree make a sharp corner with the ground, or is the base of the tree curved?

2. Cut out two small model "tree trunks" from the clear, plastic berry container. One trunk shape should be a blocky "L," made with sharp right corners. The other should be a blocky "L," but where the inside corner of the "L" is curved.

3. Hold the sharp-cornered "L" between the sunglasses on your head and a white screen on a cell phone or computer. Pull firmly outward on both ends of the "L." What do you notice?

4. Now do the same thing with the curved "L." What do you notice?

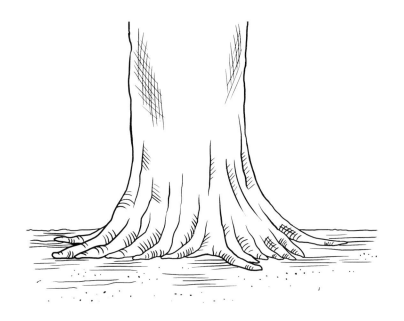

What's Going On?

When wind blows, trees get stretched on one side of their trunks. To manage the **strain** from stretching and prevent cracking, trees shape themselves using curves. When you pull on the plastic, you mimic what happens to a tree when the wind blows. The colors you see show where the strain is on the tree. In the "L" with a sharp inner corner, you can see the colors build up, showing how strain builds up in corners. But in the "L" with a curved inner corner, the colors are more spread out and not as bright, showing how curves help the strain flow through the tree without causing damage.

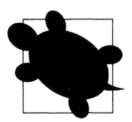

Slow Fly

What Happens to a Fly in Cold Weather?

Materials

jar with a screw-on lid

hammer

nail

live fly

adult helper

You must have access to a refrigerator.

Try This

1. Ask your adult helper to punch holes in the lid of the jar with the hammer and nail.

2. Catch a fly in the jar and screw on the lid.

3. Place the jar in the refrigerator for a few minutes.

4. Remove the jar and observe the fly.

5. Remove the lid from the jar and release the fly outside.

What's Going On?

When you placed the fly in the refrigerator, you caused its metabolism to slow down. **Metabolism** measures the rate of the chemical processes that take place in an **organism** or living thing. Metabolic processes produce energy. The metabolism of the fly was slowed by the cool temperatures in the refrigerator, so the fly did not move as quickly as it did before. After the fly warmed up, its metabolism returned to its usual rate.

Fish Skeleton

What Does the Skeleton of a Fish Do?

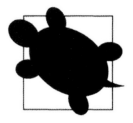

Materials

sheet of aluminum foil

fish skeleton, from a fresh fish market

magnifying lens

Try This

1. Lay the sheet of aluminum foil on a table and place the fish skeleton on it.

2. Separate the skeleton and examine the bones closely under the magnifying lens. Observe the long backbone, the individual bones, and the soft, bonelike substance that is between the bones.

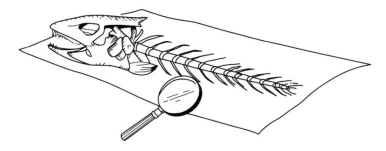

What's Going On?

Bones do many things, including providing support. Fish are called **vertebrates** because they have backbones. The backbone is made up of small, separate bones called **vertebrae**, which are separated by cushions of cartilage. **Cartilage** is a material like bone, but a little softer. You have cartilage holding up your nose. The long, sharp bones that extend from each side of the vertebra help to hold the fish's muscles in place. The backbone protects the fish's delicate and important **spinal cord.** The spinal cord, which extends from the brain along the back of the fish to the tail, is made up of nerve fibers. The sensitive nerves and cells of the spinal cord make up the nervous system, which communicate with one another to control the fish's movements. Humans have many similar bones too, because humans and fish – and all living things on Earth – are part of a big, interrelated, and interconnected family.

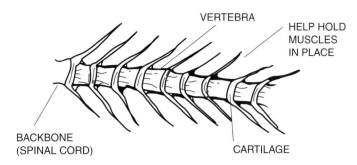

VERTEBRA

HELP HOLD MUSCLES IN PLACE

BACKBONE (SPINAL CORD)

CARTILAGE

Image by Alexas_Fotos from Pixabay

Colors

Light is mysterious, because, while we see it, we can't touch it or weigh it. The experience of **colors** results from different light waves (vibrations) bouncing off objects and reaching your eye. In a similar way, sound is a wave through the air, which we cannot touch, though we know it when we hear it.

When these vibrations of light are combined, we experience it as the color white. When light reaches an object, some vibrations are **reflected,** or bounced back, and some are **absorbed,** or taken in by the object. When you look at grass, you see green because the green light is reflected to your eye and the other colors are absorbed by the grass.

In this section, you will experiment with colors. You will mix them together and take them apart. You can even create your own rainbow.

Waves of Color

How Can You Visualize Light Waves?

Materials

regular-sized Slinky

Try This

1. Have a helper hold one end of the Slinky or fix it down by looping it on something solid.

2. Take the other end of the Slinky and walk far enough away that the Slinky is stretched out with a little bit of sag.

3. Move your arm holding the Slinky up and down to the same height at an even pace. How does the Slinky change?

4. What is causing the wave, and why does it move along the Slinky?

5. Notice the shape of the wave.

6. Notice the top of each wave, and how far it is from the top of the next wave.

7. Now move your arm holding the Slinky up and down faster, but still at the same height. Again, notice the top of each wave, and how far it is from the top of the next wave.

What's Going On?

While we can see light, the actual waves of light are too small for us to see. We can visualize them using a Slinky. The behavior of waves is similar whether we are talking about Slinkys, the ocean, sound waves, and so on. When you moved your arm up and down faster, the **wavelength**, or distance between the top of one wave and top of the next, became shorter. Our eyes and brains experience different wavelengths of light waves as different colors.

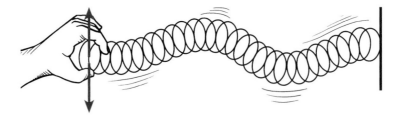

Water Rainbow
How Do Water and Sunlight Create a Rainbow?

Materials

clear plastic cup

tap water

sheet of white paper

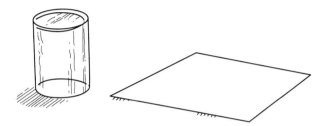

You must have access to a sunny windowsill.

Try This

1. Fill the plastic cup with tap water.

2. Place the cup of water on a windowsill in bright sunshine so the cup extends over the ledge a little. Balance the cup so it will not tip over.

3. Place the sheet of paper on the floor where the sunlight falls. What do you see on the paper?

4. Write the name of each color next to the color on the paper.

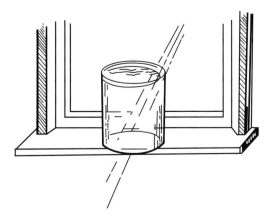

What's Going On?

A rainbow appeared on the sheet of paper. Although sunlight seems to be white, it is actually made up of a combination of all colors. As light passed through the water in the cup, the light rays of each color bent in a slightly different direction. This is because different colors have different wavelengths, which means they interact with the medium they are traveling through in differing amounts. Imagine swimming across a river. If you swim straight across, coming up for air rarely, the current of the river doesn't push you downstream that far. If you swim across just as quickly, but bob up and down more often to come up for air, the current of the river has more of an opportunity to push on your body, and you end up reaching the other bank farther downstream.

When the white light from outside passes through the water, the different color wavelengths interact with the water in differing amounts, and so turn different degrees, causing them to spread across the paper.

Notice the order of the colors of the **spectrum**, or series of color bands; and, with the aid of your paper, try and remember the order.

Oil Rainbow

What Causes the Rainbow of Colors on a Patch of Oil?

Materials

tap water

frying pan

eyedropper

vegetable oil

You must have access to a bright window.

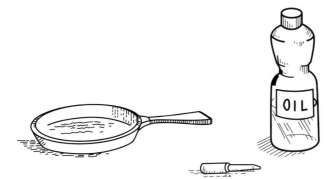

Try This

1. Pour about 1 in. (2.5 cm) depth of tap water into the pan.

2. Place the pan on a table next to a bright window. Do not place the pan in direct sunlight.

3. Look into the water at an angle so the light from the sky is reflected in your eye.

4. Observing the water from the same angle, use the eyedropper to place a drop of oil on the surface of the edge of the pan closest to you. Observe the rainbow of colors that flash away from you toward the opposite edge of the pan. Watch what happens.

5. Blow on the surface. What happens to the colors?

What's Going On?

When you first put the oil into the water, you saw a **rainbow** of colors spreading away from you toward the opposite edge of the pan. As you blew on the surface, the colors changed. The colors change because the light bounces off the oil in different places, such as the surface of the oil and the bottom of the oil, and then these waves of color interact. When waves interact, they can cancel each other out, such as when the top of one wave combines with the bottom of another wave. Or, they can make each other stronger, such as when the top of one wave joins with the top of another wave. These interacting waves determine which colors you see, and they change whenever the oil moves.

Secondary Colors

How Are Colors Made on Electronic Screens?

Materials

scissors

ruler

blue, red, and yellow pieces of acetate, from an art supply store

Try This

1. Cut two circles about 6 in. (15 cm) in **diameter** (distance across a circle) from each of the pieces of acetate.

2. Lay the acetate circles on one another to make additional colors.

3. Move the circles around to make as many different colors as you can. How many different colors can you make?

What's Going On?

Acetate is a colored transparent material that allows you to mix colors easily and temporarily. When you put the acetate circles over one another, you created different colors. The **primary colors** are red, yellow, and blue. **Secondary colors** are combinations of two primary colors. All colors, except white, can be made by mixing the primary colors. This is how electronic displays can create all the colors you see on them. Electronic displays create all the colors you see on screens using pixels containing subpixels of the three primary colors, mixed in different degrees and amounts to create a full color range.

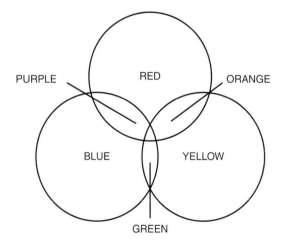

New Mix

What Happens When You Look Through Two Colors at Once?

Materials

clear plastic cup

clear plastic bowl

tap water

yellow and blue food coloring

Try This

1. Make sure the plastic cup fits inside the plastic bowl.

2. Pour tap water into the bowl until it is about three-fourths full.

3. Mix in the yellow food coloring.

4. Pour water into the cup until it is half full.

5. Mix in the blue food coloring.

6. Place the cup of blue water in the bowl of yellow water. Look through the water in the bowl at the water in the cup. What color do you see? Test other colors by changing the color of the water.

What's Going On?

The water looked green. Light is made up of a series of colored bands, the **spectrum**, which can be seen when light is broken apart by a prism. All objects reflect and absorb these colors, so the color of an object is determined by the color, or colors, that it reflects. The blue water reflected blue light and the yellow water reflected yellow light. All the other colors were absorbed by the water. By placing the cup of blue water into the bowl of yellow water, you temporarily mixed the two colors. This mixture absorbed most colors of the spectrum and reflected green light, so the water looked green.

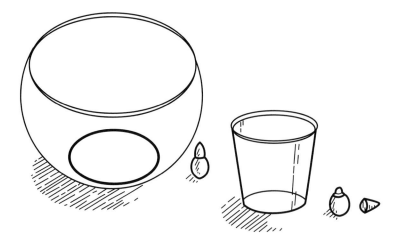

Balloon Stretch

Why Does the Color of a Balloon Become Lighter When Air Is Blown into It?

Materials

2 same-colored balloons

Try This

1. Inflate one balloon as much as you can without popping it.

2. Tie the neck of the balloon closed.

3. Hold the inflated balloon next to the balloon that is not inflated. What do you notice about the colors?

What's Going On?

Balloons are made of an elastic material called *latex* that is colored with a **pigment.** By inflating the balloon, you caused the latex to expand and become thinner. This caused the pigment in the balloon to stretch, so the color of the balloon appeared lighter.

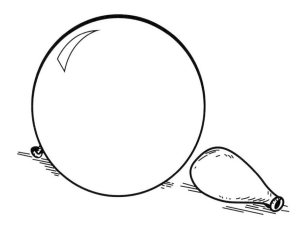

Hot Colors

How Do Colors Relate to Heat?

Materials

sheet of black construction paper

sheet of white construction paper

2 thermometers

timer

incandescent bulb or heat lamp
(optional)

Try This

1. Place both sheets of construction paper in the sun or next to the lamp.

2. Place a thermometer under each sheet.

3. Read the thermometers after 10 minutes. What is the reading of each?

What's Going On?

The **thermometer** (device for measuring temperature) under the black paper registered the higher temperature. Both sheets of paper were warmed by the sun or lamp's rays, but the white sheet reflected almost all the light that shined on it. The black paper absorbed most of the light. When light is absorbed by an object, it causes the material making up that object to vibrate more quickly. This vibration is felt by us as heat. If an object absorbs most of the light, it ends up looking black. If an object doesn't vibrate more quickly from light, then the light either bounces off the object (making it look white) or passes through it (making it look clear) and doesn't get as hot. So, it is not the color of something that causes heat, but rather, the color of an object indicates how much light it absorbs, which suggests how warm it may get in the light.

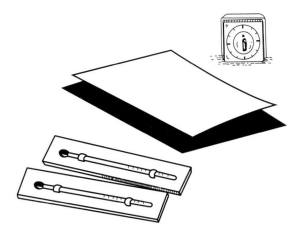

Color Dyes
How Do Fabrics Respond to Different Dye Strengths?

Materials

food coloring

2 small plastic cups

tap water

2 pieces of white cotton fabric about 2 inches (5 cm) square

2 paper towels

tweezers

Try This

1. Put two drops of the food coloring into each plastic cup.

2. Pour tap water into the first cup until it is three-fourths full.

3. Pour tap water into the second cup until it is one-third full.

4. Place one piece of the cotton fabric in each cup of colored water and let the water soak in for a few minutes.

5. Place a paper towel in front of each cup.

6. Use the tweezers to remove the pieces of fabric from the colored water. Lay each piece on a paper towel directly in front of the cup that it soaked in. What do you notice about the color of each piece of fabric?

What's Going On?

By mixing water with food coloring, you prepared a **dye** (a coloring substance). Pure food coloring is a **concentrated** (not mixed with anything) solution. When you mixed in the water, you **diluted** the color, or made it weaker. The more water you mixed in, the more the solution was diluted, and the lighter the color became. When you placed the pieces of fabric in the dye, they absorbed some of the colored water, and the fibers turned the color of the dye. The piece that was in the more diluted solution came out lighter than the one that was in the more concentrated solution.

Spinning Colors
How Does the Eye See Colors That Are Moving Very Rapidly?

Materials

ruler

pencil

cardboard or cardstock circle

red and blue marking pens

scissors

Try This

1. Use the ruler to draw a straight line through the middle of the circle from left to right and another line through the middle from top to bottom.

2. Use the marking pens to color each section of the circle, alternating colors.

3. Use the tip of the scissors to poke a hole in the middle of the circle. It should be large enough for the pencil to fit through.

4. Push the pencil point through the hole so the point is on the uncolored side.

5. Spin the pencil between your hands as you watch the colors. What happens?

What's Going On?

When you spun the circle very fast, your eyes could not see the individual colors. Instead, they saw a color that is a mix of colors on the circle. The color that you saw depended on the colors of the marking pens you used. This is why movies seem realistic to us, even though they are made up of separate pictures. The film moves too fast for our eyes to see each picture, so we see the movie as a continuously moving scene.

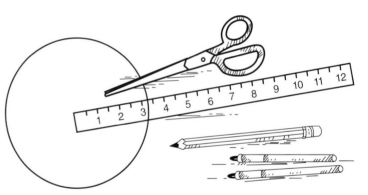

Chromatography
Can Colors Be Separated After They Have Been Mixed?

Materials

several different-colored, water-based marking pens, including orange, green, and/or purple

cone-shaped coffee filter

tap water

baking pan

Try This

1. Make as many different-colored dots as you wish on the coffee filter, keeping them about ¾ inch (15 mm) from the edge of the filter.

2. Fold the filter in half.

3. Pour tap water into the baking pan until it is about one-third full.

4. Stand the filter in the water, making sure the water does not touch any of the colored dots.

5. Observe the water move up the filter.

6. When the water has moved all the way up, remove the filter from the water and put it aside to dry. What happens to the colors?

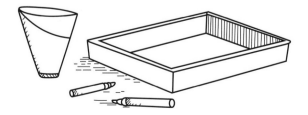

What's Going On?

Chromatography is a technique for separating chemical substances by taking advantage of the different speeds that color pigments travel in a liquid based on their size (**liquid** is matter in a state in which molecules are able to move around, but are still held in contact with the molecules around them). When you placed the coffee filter in the water, the water molecules were attracted up through the paper, which caused the pigments in the inks to travel with the water. Bigger, heavier pigments move more slowly than smaller, lighter pigments, so they separate as they flow up the filter paper. Chromatography is used by scientists to help identify the compounds in many things, including in food, liquids, medicines, substances from living things (like blood), and more.

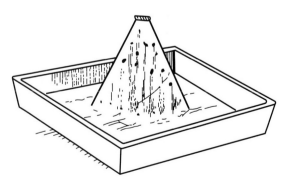

Image by Free-Photos from Pixabay

Energy

Turn on a cell phone, flip a light switch, kick a ball, or just get up in the morning, and you're using energy. **Energy** is an idea that helps us understand how physical changes – like a light bulb turning on or a volcano exploding – happen in the world. When things like this happen, energy is **converted**, or changed, from one form to another. Energy can be taken from a number of sources, including the sun, wind, running water, oil, natural gas, and even gravity.

In this section, you will explore some of the types of energy we use to do things and make our lives more comfortable. You will find out how to change one type of energy to another, and you will see how invisible energy can pop balloons and launch marshmallows.

Marshmallow Launcher
How Does Energy from a Balloon Launch Marshmallows?

Materials

paper cup

scissors

balloon

rubber band

small marshmallows

Try This

1. Eat a marshmallow.
2. Cut off the bottom of the cup.
3. Tie the end of the balloon in a knot.
4. Cut off the bottom of the balloon.
5. Stretch the balloon over the bottom of the cup.
6. Secure the balloon snugly to the bottom of the cup with a rubber band.
7. Drop a small marshmallow into the cup.
8. Pull back on the end of the balloon and let go.
9. Try to launch a marshmallow up into the air and catch it in your mouth.

What's Going On?

Our bodies can transform **stored energy** in the marshmallow into **moving energy** that runs our muscles to do things like jump, smile, and build marshmallow launchers. When you pulled back on the end of the balloon, energy from the motion of your arms transferred into the balloon. The balloon now has energy stored in it. When you let go, the balloon had moving energy, which pushed the marshmallow out of the cup. If you managed to catch a marshmallow in your mouth, you will have added energy to play more with the marshmallow launcher or do other things. Energy is moving between things around us all the time, from the sun to the Earth, from plants into animals, from people to the technologies we use. The idea of energy helps us recognize and think about these transformations.

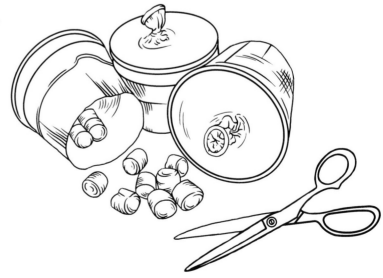

Hot Hand

How Does Friction Create Heat?

Materials

Try This

1. Hold your palm up and think about its temperature. Is your hand warm? Cold?

2. Rub the palm of your other hand quickly back and forth on your clothes or a blanket.

3. Compare how warm your hands feel to one another.

What's Going On?

When you rubbed your hand back and forth, the friction caused your skin molecules to vibrate faster. We feel this as heat. Friction causes heat and other kinds of energy to form in many ways around us. The friction between the moving parts in a computer requires a fan to cool it down, and the friction of moving air can result in lightning storms.

Different animals can feel heat in different ways. Many creatures, like certain snakes, can feel heat at a distance. Some beetles can feel the heat of a forest fire from many miles away.

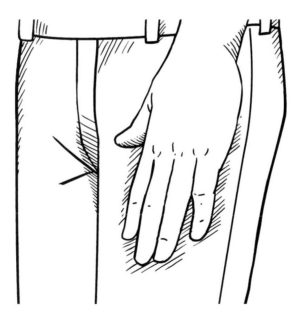

Hot Ice

How Does Pressure Affect Energy?

Materials

ice cube

paper plate

metal fork

Try This

1. Place the fork in the freezer for a few minutes.

2. Place the ice cube on the paper plate.

3. Press the fork into the ice cube and hold it there for a few minutes.

4. Remove the fork. What happens?

What's Going On?

You can see how the ice melted. The top of the ice cube melted not because the fork was warm, but because of the pressure of the fork. The pressure of the fork squeezed molecules of water closer together, which caused friction and heat energy to form. This heat melted the ice.

Spicy Music

How Does Energy Create Sound?

Materials

plastic cup

plastic wrap

rubber band

black pepper

cell phone

Try This

1. Pull the plastic wrap tight over the top of the plastic cup and secure it with the rubber band.

2. Turn on some loud music on the cell phone.

3. Place the cup on the phone's speaker.

4. Sprinkle some black pepper on the plastic wrap. Turn up the music until you see the pepper dancing.

What's Going On?

Although we can't see sound, it is created by waves passing through air molecules. In this case, the cell phone speaker moved with the music, creating waves in the air. The waves hit the plastic wrap and made it vibrate, which caused the pepper to dance around. The same thing happens when we hear: our ear drum vibrates with the sound energy that reaches it.

Sun Burst

How Powerful Is the Sun's Heat?

Materials

balloon

magnifying lens

Try This

1. Inflate the balloon and tie the neck closed.

2. Hold the magnifying lens so the sun's rays are focused directly on a spot on the balloon. Hold the lens there until the balloon pops.

What's Going On?

The sun's rays can be very strong. By using the magnifying lens, you focused or concentrated the sun's energy on one spot and intensified the heat. The heat was strong enough to melt a tiny hole in the balloon, so the balloon popped. In some places, people focus the sun's rays to cook food, or create steam to turn turbines and create electricity.

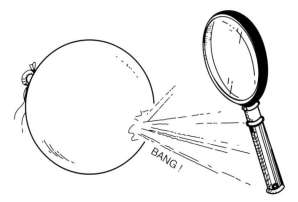

Button Spinner

How Can Energy Be Changed from One Form to Another?

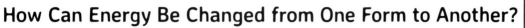

Material

3-foot (1-m) piece of string

large button with two holes

Try This

1. Lace the string through both holes in the button by going in one hole and out the other.
2. Tie the ends of the string to make large loops.
3. Move the button to the center of the string.
4. Hold one loop of the string in each hand.
5. Twirl the button toward you until the string is twisted tight.
6. Pull your hands apart and straighten the string. What happens to the button?
7. Relax the string. What happens when you continue to straighten and relax the string?

What's Going On?

When you twisted the string, you transferred energy into the string, where the energy was stored. This stored energy is also called **potential energy**. When you straightened the string, the stored energy was shifted to the button, and the button began to spin. This is energy of motion, or **kinetic energy.** The spinning button transferred the energy back to the string. As you straightened and then relaxed the string, the energy was changed back and forth between kinetic energy and potential energy. Wind-up clocks use kinetic and potential energy. When you wind a clock, you store the energy. As the energy is released, the clock runs, until the stored energy is used up.

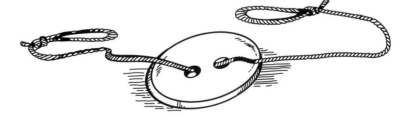

Wind Spin

How Can the Wind Produce Energy?

Materials

pencil with a flat eraser

ruler

square sheet of paper

scissors

pushpin

Try This

1. Draw a circle about 2 in. (5 cm) in diameter in the center of the sheet of paper. Put a dot in the center of the circle.

2. Cut a straight line from one corner of the sheet of paper to the circle. Be sure not to cut inside the circle. Do this for all four corners of the sheet of paper.

3. Bend every other point to the center of the circle without folding the paper. Hold the points there as you stick the pushpin through all of the points and through the center of the circle. You should have a paper windmill.

4. Gently press the pushpin into the pencil eraser.

5. Hold the paper windmill in front of you and blow on it. What happens?

What's Going On?

A wind turbine or windmill moves by the force of the wind. You powered the paper windmill by blowing on it. Windmills and turbines can be used as a source of energy. A spinning turbine can be used to turn a system of gears. **Gears** are wheels with teeth around the edges that come together and turn each other. Gears can perform a variety of jobs. Wind turbines are often used today to create electricity by moving a magnet and copper wire around each other.

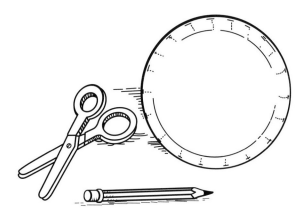

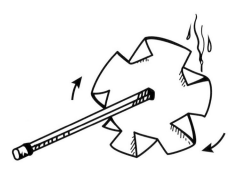

Easy Electromagnet

How Can You Make a Magnet with Electricity?

Materials

scissors

14-gauge coated wire

screwdriver

ruler

4.5-V battery

metal paper clips

adult helper

Try This

1. Ask an adult to cut a piece of the coated wire about five times as long as the metal part of the screwdriver.

2. Then your adult helper should scrape the coating off each end of the wire.

3. Leaving about 6 in. (15 cm) of wire at each end, wrap the middle portion of the wire around the metal part of the screwdriver so that the coils of wire are close together.

4. Wrap one end of the wire around one battery terminal.

5. Lay the paper clips on the table.

6. Place the tip of the screwdriver near the paper clips. What happens?

7. Wrap the free end of wire around the other battery terminal.

8. Again, hold the tip of the screwdriver near the paper clips. What happens?

9. Disconnect one wire from the battery. What happens to the paper clips now?

What's Going On?

When you connected the screwdriver to only one battery terminal and held it near the paper clips, nothing happened. When you connected the free end of the wire to the other battery terminal, electricity began flowing from the battery through the wire and around the screwdriver. The flowing electrical current causes the substance of the screwdriver to organize itself in a new way, and become a temporary magnet, an **electromagnet**. As long as the electrical current keeps flowing, the screwdriver will behave like a magnet. Electromagnets are used in many things, including in cell phones, computers, and car motors.

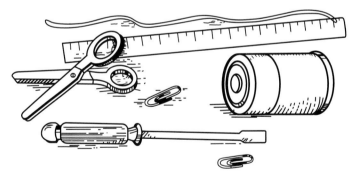

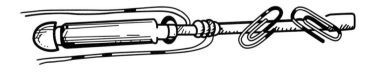

Raisin Raising

How Can the Energy in Chemicals Produce Movement?

Materials

tap water

clear plastic cup

raisins

spoon

2 tablespoons (30 ml) baking soda

2 tablespoons (30 ml) white vinegar

Try This

1. Pour tap water into the plastic cup until it is three-fourths full.

2. Drop the raisins into the cup.

3. Stir in the baking soda until it dissolves.

4. Add the vinegar. What happens?

What's Going On?

When you first put the raisins in the water, they sank to the bottom because they were heavier than the liquid (also, raisins don't know how to swim). When you added the baking soda and vinegar, these chemicals interacted, creating **carbon dioxide** gas. This gas made bubbles in the liquid, which attached themselves to the outside of the raisins. The bubbles helped lift the raisins, making them lighter than the liquid they were in, so they floated to the surface. After each raisin floated to the top, the bubbles popped and the gas went into the air. Without the bubbles, the raisins once again became heavier than the liquid and sank to the bottom to collect more bubbles.

Image by Free-Photos from Pixabay

Gravity

Gravity is a force, or power, that attracts objects to the center of the Earth. It is also one of the main forces that keeps the moon in orbit around the Earth and the Earth in orbit around the sun.

Gravity makes rivers run to the ocean and fruits fall from trees. Gravity also allows you to walk, because it acts against the energy of your steps and holds you to the planet. Without gravity, everything on Earth would float away into space. In fact, the Earth itself would fall apart and float away. Gravity is one of the most mysterious and least understood forces of Nature.

In this section, you will discover the power of gravity. You will learn how tree branches defy gravity, how tightrope walkers balance, and even why the moon revolves around the Earth.

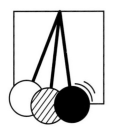

Balancing Act
What Is an Object's Center of Gravity?

Materials

ruler

Try This

1. Hold the ruler vertically with one end in the palm of your hand.

2. Let go of the ruler and balance it upright for as long as you can. Can you feel a force pulling against the ruler?

3. Turn the ruler so it is horizontal.

4. Balance the ruler by placing the middle of the ruler on your finger.

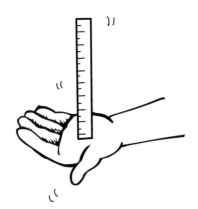

What's Going On?

The steadiness of the ruler depended on how its **weight**, or its amount of downward force, is distributed. In order to balance the ruler, you had to find the center of gravity. The **center of gravity** of an object is the point at which weight is evenly spread and all sides are in balance. It was difficult to balance the ruler when you held it vertically because half of the ruler's weight was above its center of gravity; any tilting and the ruler wanted to fall into a more stable position. When you turned the ruler to a horizontal position, you could easily balance it on your finger, because the weight was evenly distributed on either side. Tightrope walkers depend on the center of gravity to help them balance on the high wire. They hold a long pole low on their body as they walk on the rope. The pole adds weight low down, lowering their center of gravity, making it easier for them to balance.

Penny Balloon

How Can You Change the Center of Gravity of an Object?

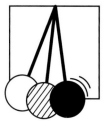

Materials

two balloons

penny

Try This

1. Stick the penny inside one balloon, blow up the balloon, and tie it off.

2. Blow up the other balloon (with no penny) and tie it off.

3. With an open palm, bounce the balloon with no penny in your hands 10 times.

4. Bounce the balloon with the penny in your hands 10 times.

What's Going On?

The balloon with no penny doesn't shift that much because its center of gravity stays the same, so it is easy to bounce in your hand. The penny in the other balloon moves around, which shifts the balloon's center of gravity, making it much more unsteady and unpredictable.

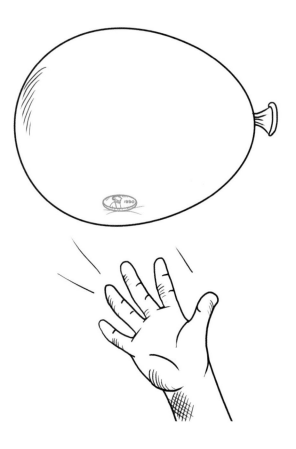

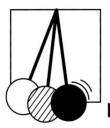

Book Balance

How Can You Make a Stack of Books Lean Without Falling Over?

Materials

6 to 8 books

Try This

1. Place one book about 1 foot (30 cm) from the edge of a table.

2. Place a second book on this book but position it to extend over the first book just enough to balance.

3. Place a third book on the second book in the same way.

4. Continue stacking the books in this way until you have used all the books. Be sure to balance the books so they do not fall over. What happens as you add books?

What's Going On?

When you stacked the books in this manner, the books acted as though they were one object and stayed as a stack until the center of gravity was no longer supported by the bottom book. As you added each book, the center of gravity changed. But as long as the center of gravity was supported, the books did not fall over. A structure anchored at one end this way is called a **cantilever**. Tree branches and apartment balconies are cantilevers. When the center of gravity was no longer supported, the books tumbled over. Structural engineers use this knowledge when they design things like bridges.

Gravity Balance

How Can You Make a Yardstick Balance at Different Points?

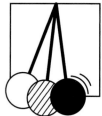

Materials

book

yardstick or meterstick

pennies

Try This

1. Open the book slightly and place it on a table, so the spine of the book is at the top.

2. Lay the yardstick (meterstick) over the spine and balance it.

3. Place one penny on one end of the stick so the stick tips.

4. Find the new center of gravity by moving the stick so it balances on the spine again.

5. Put a second penny on the opposite end of the stick. Now where is the center of gravity?

6. Continue to experiment by placing pennies at different points on the stick to find the different centers of gravity.

What's Going On?

You can balance an object by supporting it under its center of gravity. The center of gravity is exactly at the middle of the yardstick (meterstick). As you added pennies, the center of gravity moved toward the end of the stick where the pennies were. When you added an equal number of pennies on either side of the stick, the center of gravity moved back to the middle. How could you use this to determine how much something weighs?

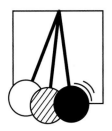

Pendulum Plus

Does the Weight of a Pendulum Affect the Timing of the Swing?

Materials

2 pieces of string about 5 ft (1.7 m) long

3 spoons

2 pushpins

adult helper

Try This

1. Tie one of the pieces of string to the thinnest part of one of the spoons.

2. Lay the other two spoons on top of each other. Tie the second piece of string to the thinnest part of the two spoons together.

3. Ask your adult helper to attach the ends of both strings to the top of a doorway with the pushpins. The strings should be about 9 in. (23 cm) apart.

4. Keeping the strings straight, pull the spoons up to the same height.

5. Release all the spoons at the same time and step back so you don't accidentally get hit. Which swings faster? Farther?

6. Now shorten the second string in half, and remove one of the spoons, before repeating steps 3–5.

What's Going On?

Pendulums are hanging weights that swing under the influence of gravity (swing sets are pendulums). When you released them, both pendulums moved back and forth at the same time with an equal amount of force. Both went back and forth to the same distance, even though one pendulum was heavier. It seems like the heavier pendulum should swing faster, but all objects accelerate the same amount when freely falling. When you shortened the string of one pendulum, it swung faster because the string's momentum from gravity only allowed it to go a certain distance away before gravity pulled it back.

Imagine the strings were tied loosely around a tree limb. With enough energy, the spoons would go around and round the tree limb. Similarly, the moon circles around the Earth. The pulling force of the Earth's gravity is balanced by the outward force the moon feels swinging around our planet.

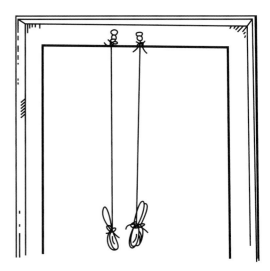

Paper Plunge
Does Shape Influence Gravity?

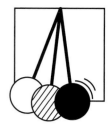

Materials

two pieces of identical notebook paper

Try This

1. Crumple both pieces of paper into a ball.
2. Hold each ball of crumpled paper in outstretched arms.
3. Drop the papers at the same time and observe when each hits the ground.
4. Unfold one ball of paper so it is flat. Hold it parallel to the floor while completing step #3 again.

What's Going On?

Gravity appears to act on the crumpled piece of paper more strongly than on the flattened piece of paper. But both pieces of paper are the same weight, and when they were both crumpled, they reached the ground at about the same time. Instead, what is happening is that the flattened piece of paper encounters more air molecules during its fall than the crumpled one, which bump into the paper before getting out of the way and slow the paper's descent. Shape and size may appear to influence gravity, but it is air resistance instead. If you repeated this activity on the moon holding a hammer and a feather, which one do you think would hit the ground first?

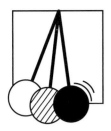

Gravity Pull
Why Don't Liquids Flow at the Same Rate?

Materials

paper hole-punch

3 paper cups

masking tape

large pan

molasses or honey

tap water

vegetable oil

timer

helper

Try This

1. Punch a hole in the side of each paper cup near the bottom. Be sure the holes in all the cups are the same size and the same distance from the bottom.

2. Place a small piece of masking tape over the hole in each cup.

3. Place the cups in the large pan.

4. Pour the molasses (or honey), tap water, and vegetable oil each into a separate cup up to the top.

5. With your helper, remove the tape from the cups all at the same time. Note the amount of time it takes each liquid to run out of each cup. In what order do the cups empty?

What's Going On?

Gravity acts on each liquid the same, so why does each cup empty at different speeds? The first cup to empty was the one filled with water. The last cup to empty was the one filled with molasses/honey. While gravity pulls on everything with the same force, different liquids can flow at different rates. The **viscosity** of a liquid is the rate at which the liquid can be poured. One of the thickest of all liquids is Silly Putty.

Image by Alex Tse from Pixabay

The Human Body

The **human body** is a wondrous, complex organism made up of many different parts that all work together to help you function every day. Each cell in your body plays a vital role. The skeletal system supports your body with its detailed structure of bones. Your muscular system helps you move. Your circulatory system helps keep blood and other fluids moving to bring nutrients to all your cells. And your skin helps keep all of these systems inside your body and protect you.

In this section, you will discover much more about your body and how it functions. You will make an instrument for listening to your heart. You will tease your eyes with illusions. And you will even hear your bones growing.

Pulse Watch

How Can You Tell Your Heart Is Beating?

Materials

toothpick

modeling clay

Try This

1. Stick the toothpick into a small ball of the modeling clay.

2. Hold your arm straight out, keeping it perfectly still.

3. Place the ball of clay with the tooth-pick facing up on the area of your wrist where you think your pulse is located. You may need to move the ball around until you find the strongest beat. What happens to the toothpick?

What's Going On?

You have a river inside you: the blood in your body flows through a complicated network, bringing nutrients and oxygen to all the cells in your body. The toothpick moved as your blood was pumped on its long trip through your blood vessels to your heart. Your **pulse** beat because your heart is a muscle that pumps blood into the arteries for circulation through your blood vessels. Doctors measure pulse rates to find out if a person's heart is beating normally.

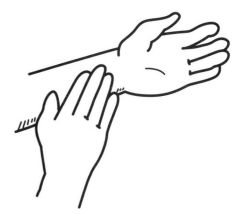

Pulse Change

How Does Your Heart Know When to Speed Up?

Materials

stopwatch or watch with second hand

Try This

1. Find your pulse by putting the tips of your index and middle finger on your wrist.

2. Count how many times your heart beats in 15 seconds.

3. Now run in place or do jumping jacks for 30 seconds.

4. Count how many times your heart beats in 15 seconds.

What's Going On?

To move your body, your muscle cells break down molecules of food you ate earlier to create energy. The waste products of those molecules are released into the blood stream. Sensors in the walls of your blood stream detect these molecules and send a signal to your brain, which sends a signal to your heart to beat faster. This brings your muscle cells more nutrients and oxygen that they need to keep working. This kind of system is known as a **feedback loop**, and it is an important way our bodies know how to adapt to changes.

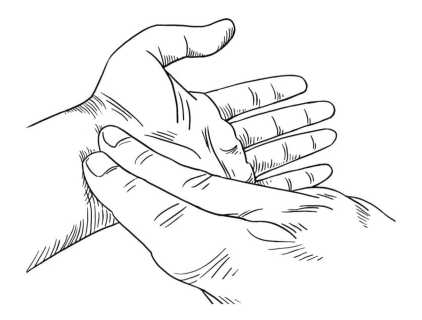

Heart Sounds

How Can You Hear Your Heart?

Materials

plastic funnel

cardboard tube from a paper towel roll

duct tape

Try This

1. Place the cardboard tube over the smaller end of the funnel and tape it securely in place.

2. Place the funnel over a willing volunteer's chest. What do you hear?

What's Going On?

You heard your heart pumping blood with this model of a stethoscope. A **stethoscope** is a device that captures sound waves and channels them down a tube directly into your ear so you can better hear sounds of the body. Your heart beats more than 100 000 times in a single day!

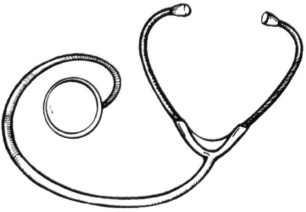

Muscle Bound

How Do Muscles Work?

Materials

Try This

1. Place one hand over the muscles on the upper part of your arm and hold it there.

2. Move the lower part of your arm back and forth. What do you feel?

What's Going On?

Muscles are the part of your body that help you move. You're using eye muscles right now, just to read this. Muscles usually work in pairs. When you moved your arm, you felt your **biceps** and **triceps** working. Muscles like the biceps and triceps work when your brain tells them to. But other muscles move without instructions from your brain. For example, the heart is a muscle, but you do not need to tell it to pump.

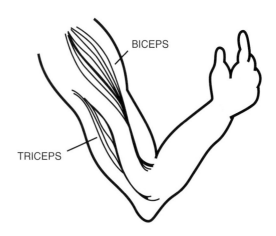

BICEPS

TRICEPS

Bone Brilliance

How Do Bones Know How to Change?

Materials

a quiet place

Try This

1. Place the palms of your hands over your ears.

2. Squeeze your hands inward until your arm muscles flex, as though you were trying to squash your head. Keep squeezing and hold this position. What do you hear?

What's Going On?

Bones are alive, just like your skin and heart, because they are made of living cells. Bones grow as you grow, but they don't just adjust as you get taller and bigger. They also change size and shape depending on how much you need their support. Tennis players, for example, have arm bones that are larger on one side of their body (their dominant side), because that's the arm they use to swing the tennis racket.

When you push on your ears, the muscles in your arms start vibrating very quickly. This sounds like a low rumble. These muscle movements tell your bones to start adding more bone material in these areas, because they are getting more use. In a way, you are hearing your own bones grow.

Eye Light
How Do You See in the Dark?

Materials

mirror

Try This

1. Look closely at one of your eyes in the mirror.

2. Notice the black spot at the center of the eye and the area around it.

3. Close your eyes for a few minutes. Then open them and look at the area around the black spot again. What does this area do when more light strikes it?

What's Going On?

When you first opened your eyes after you had closed them for a while, your pupil was large, but then it immediately became smaller as the light struck it. Light enters your eye through the little black spot called the **pupil**. Around the pupil is the colored part, known as the **iris**. If the light is dim, the pupil expands and lets more light in. This helps you see better in the dark. If the light is bright, the pupil contracts and shuts out some light, to reduce glare.

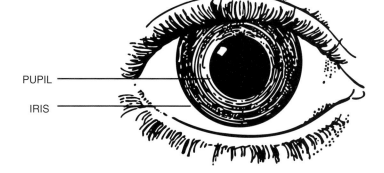

PUPIL

IRIS

Weird Wonder

What Happens If You Stare at One Color for a Long Time?

Materials

pencil

ruler

2 sheets of white paper

yellow, green, and black marking pens

timer

Try This

1. Draw a 6-in. (15-cm) square on one sheet of paper.

2. Draw a 1-in. (2.5-cm) yellow border around the square.

3. Color the area within the border green.

4. Put a black dot in the center of the square.

5. In bright light, hold up the paper and stare at the black dot for about one minute without blinking.

6. When time is up, look at the blank sheet of paper. What do you see?

What's Going On?

You saw an image of the square on the blank sheet of paper, but in different colors. Special parts of your eyes, called **cones**, distinguish among green, red, and blue light. These are the three primary colors that make up white light. When you stared at the black dot for a minute, the cones corresponding to that color worked continuously. When you later stared at the blank white paper, which is made up of three colors, only the cones that were not working earlier worked, because the others had been overworked.

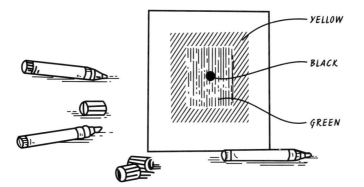

YELLOW

BLACK

GREEN

Crying Eyes

Why Do Onions Make You Weep?

Materials

onion

Try This

1. Close one of your eyes and keep it closed.

2. Peel some layers off an onion. Scratch the onion with your fingernail. What happens to your open eye?

3. How does your closed eye feel? Now open it.

What's Going On?

Onions are part of a plant. The onion part we eat is called a **bulb**. The plant makes a bulb to store food for itself, to use later.

When you peeled the onion, your eye began to tear. Onions contain an irritating chemical that escapes into the air when the onion is damaged. When the chemical reaches your eyes, they start to water and sting. Why do you think onions have such a chemical that gets released when they're injured? (Hint: Remember what onions use their bulb for.)

Old Shoes

Why Do Shoes Wear Out in Different Places?

Materials

pair of old shoes

rubber band, about 3 in. long

mirror

Try This

1. Loop the rubber band over your thumb and index finger. Push your fingers down on a tabletop so they spread apart. Try this a few times.

2. Examine the sole of each shoe for places where it has worn thin. Look at the heels. Look at the toe area of each shoe.

3. Now look at the bottom of your foot in a mirror. Notice the heel, area just below the toes (the toe ball), and the space between your heel and the ball of your toes.

What's Going On?

There is an arch in the bones of your foot. Soft tissue spans the sole of your foot, connecting one end of the boney arch (your heel) to the other end (the balls of your toes). The soft tissue here is stretchy, like a rubber band. Each time your foot contacts the ground as you walk, the tissues stretch, storing energy from pushing down, then relax, releasing some energy back into your legs.

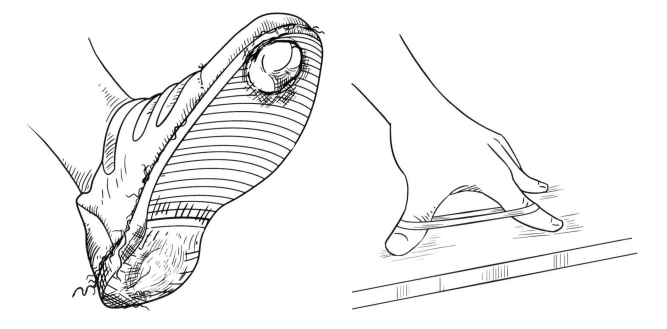

When you examined your shoes, you noticed that they were worn in some places more than in others. The heel and toe ball area are where you exert the most pressure, causing the shoe to wear down here more. But the middle of the shoe sole is less worn down, because the other parts of your foot protect the important and useful soft, stretchy tissue as you walk.

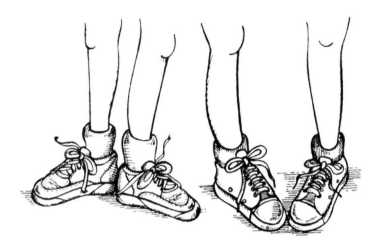

All Together Now

How Closely Related Are We to Other Creatures?

Materials

picture of the hand of a chimpanzee (e.g., from the Internet)

Try This

1. Look closely at your own hand. Notice the structure of it, the fingernails, the creases of the skin.

2. Find a picture of the hand of a chimpanzee and look closely at it.

What's Going On?

People are very closely related to other forms of Life on this planet, such as chimpanzees. Sometimes what we focus on is differences. But when we pay attention to certain details, sometimes what becomes clear are the similarities. Just like people can have brothers, sisters, and cousins, the other forms of Life that we share this planet with are our relatives. Life is one very big family.

Image by strikers from Pixabay

Light

Light is a unique phenomenon. The biggest source of light in our world is the Sun. The Sun is a star, just like all the stars you see at night. The Sun is what stars look like when they're up close.

Light travels in waves through space. Although light travels very quickly, distances in space are very large. When the sun rises, the light you see was emitted from the sun several minutes earlier. When you look at the stars at night, you're seeing light that often was emitted thousands of years ago. You see objects because light reflects from them. Light also magnifies, bends, and bounces.

In this section, you will discover why the Moon looks the way it does at different times of the month and why the sky looks blue. You will even make a simple kaleidoscope using objects you collect.

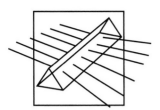

Tiny Mirror

How Does a Spoon Reflect Images?

Materials

two shiny, metal spoons

Try This

1. Hold one spoon up by the handle and look at its backside (the part that curves outward).

2. Turn the spoon horizontally and look at your image now. How does your image change?

3. Hold up the other spoon next to the first, but look at its frontside (the part that curves inward). Now what do you see?

What's Going On?

When you held the spoon vertically by the handle looking at the backside, you saw a long, thin image of yourself. When you turned the spoon sideways, or horizontally, you saw a short, wide image. When you looked into the bowl (frontside) of the spoon, you saw an upside-down image of yourself. A spoon is both convex — bending outward — and concave — bending inward. A flat mirror reflects, or bounces, light straight back to your eye. Since a spoon is curved on the backside, the light reflected off you onto the spoon becomes spread out, or squeezed together, changing the shape of your image. In the bowl of the spoon, the light reflecting off you hits one part of the bowl and gets reflected to the opposite side of the bowl, before being reflected back to your eye. Your image gets flipped over.

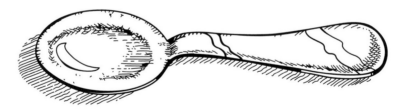

Bending Straws

What Happens to Light When It Travels Through Water?

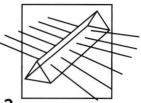

Materials

clear cup

tap water

drinking straw

Try This

1. Fill the cup with tap water.

2. Place the drinking straw in the cup.

3. Bend down to look at the straw through the side of the cup. What do you notice about the straw?

What's Going On?

When you looked at the straw from the side, it appeared to be broken, but it really was not. Light is going through two different materials here, air and water. When this happens, the light rays bend or **refract**. Light travels faster in air than in water, so the light rays get deflected more in the water. This changes where the image of the straw appears to be reflected from. The continuous straw now looks like it has a break in it.

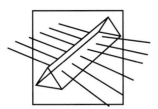

Light Beams
Why Does Light Make the Sky Look Blue?

Materials

clear plastic cup

tap water

milk

flashlight

Try This

1. Fill the plastic cup with tap water.

2. Darken the room.

3. Shine a beam of light from the flashlight through the water.

4. Turn on the room light and add a few drops of milk so the water becomes a little cloudy.

5. Darken the room again.

6. Hold the flashlight in front of the cup so the beam shines through.

7. Look into the plastic cup from above. What happens to the milk?

What's Going On?

When you shine light through the water, the light passes through it. When you added the milk drops to the water, some of the colors in light reflected back to your eyes. The light in the milky water turned pale blue because blue vibrations of light reflect more easily than other colors in light. Dust and drops of water are almost always in the Earth's atmosphere. These particles reflect blue light while other colors pass through the sky, making the sky light up blue whenever the sun shines. When the sun rises or sets, the colors change because the light has to pass through more particles at different angles, so other light waves are bent toward your eyes.

Even during the day, the nighttime sky is still right there. Without an atmosphere to reflect certain colors of light to our eyes, we would see a black sky full of stars, even during the daytime.

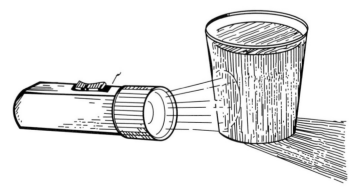

Stick Mirror

Can You See Around Corners?

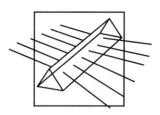

Materials

yardstick (meterstick)

masking tape

pocket mirror

to be performed in front of a doorway

Try This

1. Lay the yardstick (meterstick) on a table.

2. Tape the top and bottom of the pocket mirror to one end of the stick. Be sure not to cover the reflective surface of the mirror.

3. Turn the mirror and stick over and tape the back to secure it better.

4. Stand on one side of a doorway and use the stick to hold the mirror out the door opening. Move the mirror around to see different objects in the environment.

What's Going On?

You made a simple **periscope**, an instrument that lets you see objects around a corner. The light reflected off the mirror at the same angle at which it struck the mirror. If you held the mirror at the right angle, you could reflect the light rays coming through the door into your eyes, so you could see what was around the corner. Submarines use periscopes to look over the surface of the ocean. Dentists use angled mirrors to see around your teeth.

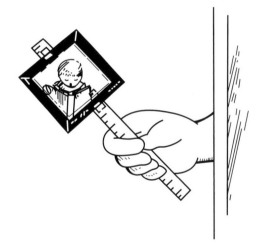

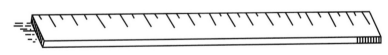

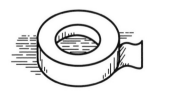

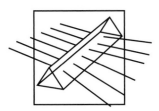

Easy Kaleidoscope

How Can Reflections Be Multiplied to Make Interesting Geometric Shapes?

Materials

3 rectangular pocket mirrors

masking tape

tiny objects (seeds, stones, pieces of paper)

Try This

1. Arrange the three pocket mirrors so they stand on the short end and face one another. The mirrors should form a triangle with the mirrored sides facing in.

2. Fasten the backs of the mirrors together with the masking tape.

3. Drop the tiny objects into the space created by the mirrors and look through the opening at the top. What do you see?

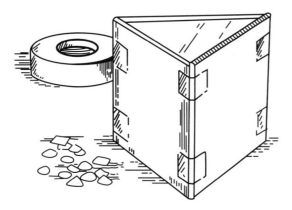

What's Going On?

You made your own **kaleidoscope**. Light in the kaleidoscope reflected from mirror to mirror, creating repeated images and patterns. When you changed the position of the objects in the kaleidoscope, new patterns of images were created.

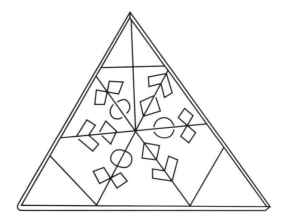

Infinite Mirrors
Does Light Go On Forever?

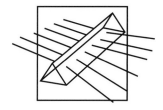

Materials

one pocket mirror and one wall mirror

Try This

1. Stand in front of a wall mirror.

2. Hold the pocket mirror up near your eyes, facing away from you, so that it is pointed at the other mirror. How many mirrors do you count?

What's Going On?

Light reflects off one mirror into another mirror, which reflects this light back again, and so on. In theory, the light causing these reflections goes on forever. We know this because light in space, without anything blocking it, travels enormous distances. Telescopes have observed light from a galaxy 13 billion light-years away from Earth. In other words, this light has traveled for 13 billion years without stopping!

Comb Beams

How Do the Angles of the Sun's Rays Affect Their Strength?

Materials

comb

piece of white cardboard

Try This

1. Place the comb with the teeth down next to one edge of the piece of cardboard so the rays of the sun shine through the teeth onto the cardboard.

2. Tilt the cardboard to different angles, always leaving the bottom edge next to the teeth on the table. How does the angle of the cardboard affect the light pattern on the cardboard?

What's Going On?

Light can spread out or be concentrated to cover large or small areas. Depending on the way you tilted the cardboard, the sun's rays coming through the comb were either lengthened or shortened. When the light covered a large area, it was not as bright, because it was not as strong in any one spot on the cardboard as was the direct light. Because the Earth is tilted in relation to the sun, light from the sun strikes the Earth at different angles during the year. We have summer in our northern **hemisphere** when this half of the Earth is tilted toward the sun and the light rays shine on it more directly. When it is winter in the northern hemisphere, the light rays hit Earth at more of an angle and are spread out.

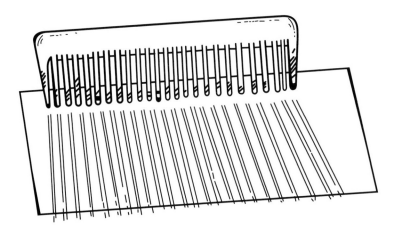

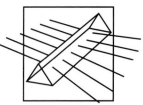

Moon Phases

How Does the Sun Create the Patterns of Light Reflections We See on the Moon?

Materials

soft round ball, like a tennis ball or round piece of foam

sharp pencil

bare light bulb at eye level, e.g., from a lamp

a room that can get dark

Try This

1. Push the pencil through the bottom of the ball.

2. In a dark room with the light bulb on, hold the ball between you and the light bulb. What do you see?

3. Slowly move the ball in a wide circle around the light bulb to the left, watching the pattern of light on the ball as you go.

What's Going On?

The light reflecting off the Moon changes shape throughout each month. When the ball was between you and the light bulb, the side of the ball facing you was dark. Likewise, when the Moon is between the Earth and Sun, the Moon cannot be seen on Earth, and it is called the New Moon (when the Moon is in a direct line between the Earth and Sun, this is a solar eclipse). When the ball was directly opposite this position, with the light bulb between you and the ball, you could see one-half of the ball. When the Moon is in this position, it is known as the Full Moon (When the Earth is directly between the Sun and Moon, it is a lunar eclipse.). In between these two positions, the Moon is lit up either on its right or left side. When the right side is lit, the light of the Moon is growing, soon to be full. When the left side is lit, the light of the Moon is leaving, and it will soon be a New Moon.

Image by Gabor Fejes from Pixabay

Machines

Machines are devices that make work easier. They can be simple, like a hammer, or very complex, like a computer. With machines, people can perform many tasks they might not otherwise be able to do as easily or at all.

In this section, you will create a variety of useful and fun machines. You will make a simple submarine, a clock, and a machine that can move objects across the room so you do not need to get up.

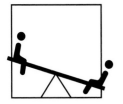

Lever Lift

How Can a Lever Help Lift Objects?

Materials

book

ruler

Try This

1. Place the book on a table so the edge is against the edge of the table.

2. Use your index finger to lift up the book.

3. Now place the ruler under the book so the ruler extends over the edge of the table.

4. Pressing down again with your index finger, slowly press on the part of the ruler that extends over the edge of the table. What happens to the book? Which method of lifting the book took more effort?

What's Going On?

When you pressed on the ruler, you lifted the book. It probably felt a lot easier to do than lifting the book directly. By using the ruler, you created a simple machine called a lever. A **lever** is a straight, stiff object, like the ruler, that **pivots** (turns) at a point called the **fulcrum** (in this case, the edge of the table). Levers allow you to move an object using less force than you would need to move the object directly. When you push one end of the lever down, the other end moves up with the same amount of force. The closer the fulcrum is to the object you want lifted, the easier it is to lift the object, because the distance that the end of the lever has to travel becomes very short for the thing you want lifted. Crowbars, nutcrackers, and even seesaws are levers. It is easier to lift your friend up on a seesaw than in your arms. If your friend moves closer to the middle of the seesaw, your friend is even easier to lift.

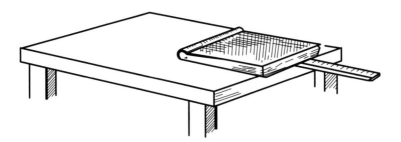

Easy Move

How Can Wheels Be Used to Decrease Friction?

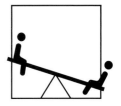

Materials

2 books

5 pencils

Try This

1. Place one book on a table.

2. Place the five pencils on the table and place the other book on the pencils.

3. Push each book with one finger to move it. Which book was easier to move?

What's Going On?

The book that was on the pencils was easier to move. The pencils acted as wheels, reducing the amount of **friction** (resistance to motion) between the book and the table. There was less friction on the pencils than on the book because a smaller part of the surface of the pencils was touching the table.

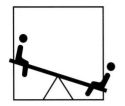

Sinking Submarine
How Does a Submarine Float and Sink?

Materials

2-liter soda bottle with cap

tub of tap water

Try This

1. Place the soda bottle with the cap screwed on in the tub of tap water. What happens to the bottle?

2. Remove the bottle from the water.

3. Fill the bottle with water and screw the cap back on.

4. Again, place the bottle in the tub of water. What happens now?

What's Going On?

When you first put the bottle in the tub, it floated. After you filled the bottle with water, it sank to the bottom of the tub. A submarine uses air and water in special tanks, called **ballast tanks**, to move up and down in the water. To dive, the submarine's tanks are filled with water. To rise, the tanks are filled with compressed air, which pushes out the water. A combination of air and water allows the submarine to stay at different depths of water. Fish use a similar method to swim at different depths in the ocean.

Simple Siphon
How Does a Siphon Work?

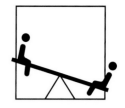

Materials

scissors

plastic tubing

2 plastic bowls

2 or 3 books

tap water

food coloring

Try This

1. Cut a piece of the plastic tubing about as long as your arm.

2. Place the first bowl on the books.

3. Pour tap water into the first bowl and add a few drops of food coloring.

4. Place the second bowl on the table. The tubing should reach from one bowl to the other.

5. Place one end of the tubing in the colored water. Suck on the free end of the tubing until all the air is removed and the tubing is full of water. Hold your tongue over the end of the tubing to keep the water in place.

6. Carefully remove the end of the tubing from your mouth and hold your finger over the end as soon as your tongue lets go.

7. Place the end of the tubing in the second bowl.

8. Remove your finger. What happens?

What's Going On?

When you removed your finger from the end of the tubing, the water steadily flowed from the upper bowl to the lower bowl. This is how a siphon works. The water kept moving through the tubing once it started because the pressure of the air on the water in the upper bowl pushed the water down the tubing. The weight of the water in the long end of the tubing also pulled the water down. Also, water is attracted to itself; hence, as it flows out, it pulls the water behind it, like a train of elephants holding each other's tails.

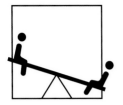

Sand Clock

How Can You Make a Simple Clock?

Materials

two 2-liter soda bottles with caps

hammer

fat nail

sand

masking tape

timer

marking pen

adult helper

Try This

1. Ask your adult helper to put the soda bottle caps on top of each other and punch a hole through the center of both, using the hammer and nail. The holes should match perfectly.

2. Fill one bottle with the sand.

3. Place a cap on each bottle.

4. Hold the empty bottle upside down on top of the full bottle and tape the caps together tightly.

5. Flip the bottles so the bottle with the sand is on top.

6. Watch the sand begin to sift through to the empty bottle. Time how long it takes the sand to go through the bottle caps. Put a mark on the outside of the bottle at the sand level every 10 minutes.

What's Going On?

You made a simple sand clock. The sand slowly moved through the cap of one bottle and through the other cap. The sand clock worked because sand always takes the same amount of time to flow through the hole. Many years ago, sand clocks were made by using glass bulbs. The sand flowed from one bulb to the other. They were called **hourglasses**, because it took exactly one hour for the sand to fall from one bulb into the other.

Turning Time

How Do Gears Work?

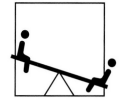

Materials

2 large brass fasteners

large empty thread spool

small empty thread spool

piece of heavy cardboard

ruler

strong rubber band

marking pen

Try This

1. Put a brass fastener through the holes of each thread spool.

2. Use the fasteners to attach each spool to the piece of cardboard 6 in. (15 cm) apart.

3. Stretch the rubber band around both spools so it is tight.

4. Mark a dot on the top edge of each spool. Turn one spool at a time and watch what happens to the other spool.

5. See how much you have to move one spool to make the other turn a complete rotation.

What's Going On?

The diameter, or the distance across, of the small spool is smaller than that of the large spool. Therefore, you had to turn the small spool several times to make the large spool turn once. When machines use big wheels to move small wheels, the small wheels turn faster. When small wheels move large ones, the large wheels turn more slowly, but have more power. Gears are wheels that have teeth along the rims. The teeth fit into the spaces between the teeth in other gears, so when one gear turns, so do the others. See how big and small wheels work together by looking at your bike and its gears. How do the different combination of gears change the effort needed to ride uphill?

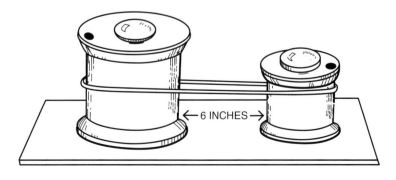

6 INCHES

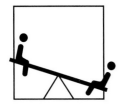

Pulling Pulleys

How Can You Use Pulleys to Move Objects Across a Room?

Materials

2 wire clothes hangers

2 empty toilet tissue tubes

piece of string the length of the distance between the doorknobs, plus 6 in. (15 cm)

large paper clip

tiny basket

adult helper

You must have access to two doors with doorknobs across the room from each other.

Try This

1. Ask your adult helper to unwind both wire hangers and slip one wire hanger through each of the toilet tissue tubes.

2. Wind the wires as they were originally.

3. Suspend each hanger on a doorknob.

4. Lace the piece of string around both tubes (where the toilet tissue was once wrapped) and pull the string so it is tight.

5. Bring the two ends of the string together and tie them in a knot. Cut off the ends of the string.

6. Bend the paper clip into a hook that has an S shape.

7. Place the S hook on the string and tighten it around the string.

8. Hang the basket on the bottom of the S hook.

9. Place small, lightweight items in the basket.

10. Pull the string. What happens to the basket?

What's Going On?

You created a pulley system to transport lightweight objects. A **pulley** is a simple machine made from a wheel and a string or rope that helps move and lift objects. The wheel helps support the weight of the object being moved. Also, a second wheel reduces the weight on any of the pulleys by half, just like carrying a heavy object with a friend holding one side.

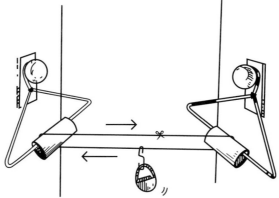

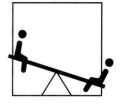

Pull Ups
How Can a Pulley Help Lift Objects?

Materials

2 wire clothes hangers

2 empty toilet tissue tubes

tap water

plastic shopping bag (without holes)

piece of string

adult helper

Try This

1. Ask your adult helper to unwind both clothes hangers and slip one wire hanger through each empty toilet tissue tube.

2. Wind the wires as they were originally.

3. Suspend each hanger on a tree branch or horizontal pole.

4. Pour tap water into the plastic bag.

5. Try lifting the water-filled bag with your arm.

6. Now lace the piece of string around the tubes (where toilet tissue was once wrapped) and tie one end to the handles of the plastic bag.

7. Pull down on the other end of the string. What happens?

What's Going On?

The pulley made it easier for you to pull up the plastic bag of water. The top pulley helped support the bag's weight. The pulleys also changed the direction of the force needed to lift the water: it is easier to pull down than lift up.

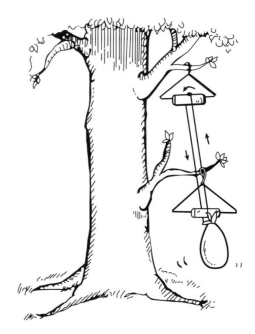

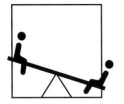

Ramp Marbles

How Can Ramps Make Lifting Easier?

Materials

large 3-ring notebook

small sealable bag

handful of marbles

Try This

1. Lay the notebook flat on a table.

2. Put the marbles in the bag and seal it.

3. Place the bag on the table next to the spine of the binder.

4. Pinch the top of the bag between your thumb and index finger and lift it to the top of the spine.

5. Now hold the bag the same way and drag it from the table up the inclined side of the notebook, to the spine.

What's Going On?

When you used the inclined side of the notebook, it took longer to get the marbles to the top, but it felt easier along the way. The ramp supported the weight of the marbles and got the bag to where it needed to go. Ramps do not actually reduce the amount of energy required to lift something, but they spread the effort over a longer distance. This reduces the amount of effort required to do something at any one moment. Ramps are sometimes found hiding in plain sight. A screw, for example, goes into wood more easily than a nail. The threads of a screw are like a spiral ramp, which makes twisting into wood easier.

Lars Plougmann/Flickr

Magnetism

Some objects behave very strangely around each other, pulling closer together or farther apart, all on their own. **Magnets** behave this way because the many tiny, invisible moving parts inside magnets are all vibrating in parallel with each other. In non-magnets, these parts are moving in many different directions at the same time.

Through the experiments and activities in this section, you will be able to "see" invisible magnetic force fields surrounding magnets. You will discover what objects magnets can attract, and you will see how the Earth itself is one giant, planet-sized magnet.

Making Moves

How Do the Ends of Magnets Affect Each Other?

Materials

2 bar magnets

Try This

1. Lay both magnets on a table.

2. Slowly slide one end of the first magnet toward one end of the second. What happens?

3. Slowly slide the other end of the second magnet near the same end of the first magnet. What do you feel this time?

What's Going On?

The ends of a magnet behave differently from one another. Magnets have **poles**, called "north" and "south," where the magnetic forces are concentrated. When placed near each other, the same, or "like," ends of magnets **repel** (push away) each other, whereas the opposite ends **attract** (pull toward) each other. When you moved the two like ends of the magnets close together, you felt the strong repelling force. When you moved the opposite ends close together, the magnets reached a point where they quickly attached to each other. The ends of all magnets behave this way. If we cut a magnet in half, the new ends too would behave this way.

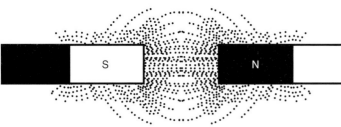

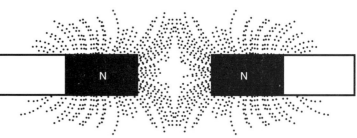

Force Fields

What Do Magnetic Forces Look Like?

Materials

2 bar magnets

4 sheets of paper

iron filings, from a store that sells equipment for scientific experiments

ruler

Try This

1. Place a piece of paper on the table. Pour some iron filings on it.

2. Place one bar magnet on a table.

3. Put a sheet of paper over the magnet.

4. Sprinkle some iron filings on the sheet. What shape do the filings take?

5. Sprinkle some iron filings farther away from the magnet. Do these take on the same shape?

6. Remove the paper carefully and place the two magnets about 4 in. (10 cm) apart. The north pole of one should face the south pole of the other.

7. Place a sheet of paper on the magnets and sprinkle some iron filings on the sheet. What shape do the filings take this time?

8. Remove the paper carefully and place the two magnets with their north poles facing each other and positioned about 4 in. (10 cm) apart.

9. Place a sheet of paper on the magnets and sprinkle some iron filings on the sheet. What shape do the filings take?

What's Going On?

We know that magnets can have an effect (exert a force) on things around them, even without touching. We can observe more about this strange force field using these tiny pieces of metal. The patterns of the iron filings help us visualize the magnetic fields around magnets. The lines you saw are called the **lines of force**, and they never cross one another. Magnetic fields extend a limited distance from a magnet. The pattern in lines in the field around a magnet can reveal which poles attract each other and which repel each other.

Flying Paper Clip
How Can You Make a Paper Clip Levitate?

Materials

small steel paper clip

thread about 6 in. long (15 cm)

small piece of tape

bar magnet

Try This

1. Tie the thread to the paper clip.

2. Tape the other end of the string to something stationary, like a table, so that the paper clip dangles off the edge.

3. Hold the magnet above the paper clip a little farther away than the length of the thread.

What's Going On?

When a magnet gets near certain non-magnetic metals, the magnetic field of the magnet flows through the metal. This causes the metal's moving parts to start moving in the same direction as the magnet and become attracted to the magnet. Magnets can be used to make things levitate. Some trains use magnets to levitate them over a track and travel with little friction.

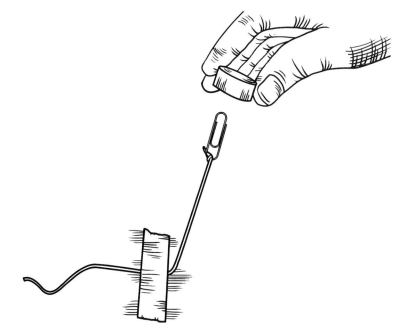

New Magnet

How Can You Make a Magnet?

Materials

large iron nail or needle

iron filings, from a store that sells equipment for scientific experiments

magnet

Try This

1. Hold the nail near the iron filings. What happens?
2. Rub the nail with the magnet about 75 times, stroking in one direction only.
3. Again, hold the nail next to the iron filings. What happens?

What's Going On?

When you first put the nail near the iron filings, nothing happened. After you rubbed the nail with the magnet, the nail picked up the iron filings. The magnet's field makes the moving parts that make up the nail line up and move in the same direction. This makes the nail acquire magnetic behaviors, just like the magnet. If you try to use the nail as a magnet later, it will no longer be magnetic. The nail's moving parts have fallen back out of alignment. Some magnets are permanently magnetic, while others are temporary.

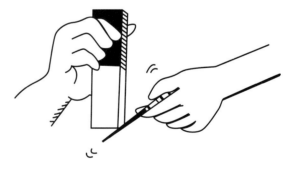

Homemade Compass

How Can You Make a Compass?

Materials

bar magnet

needle

plastic dish

tap water

knife (to be handled by an adult)

cork

adult helper

Try This

1. Rub one end of the bar magnet against the needle about 75 times, stroking in one direction only.

2. Fill the plastic dish with tap water.

3. Ask your adult helper to slice off a thin piece of the cork.

4. Float the cork in the water and lay the needle on top of it. Where does the needle point?

What's Going On?

Our entire planet is actually a giant magnet. Like all magnets, the Earth has a magnetic field, with one pole near its axis of rotation near the North Pole, and the other in Antarctica. A **compass** is an instrument that detects the Earth's magnetic field. The south pole of a magnetic needle is attracted to the north pole of the Earth, so it points to the north. By rubbing the bar magnet across the needle, you turned the needle into a magnet. The water allowed the needle to move freely. Because the Earth's magnetic field doesn't usually change much, people have used compasses for hundreds of years to help orient themselves when traveling. Many other creatures orient themselves using the Earth's magnetic field too, although how exactly they achieve this is yet unknown.

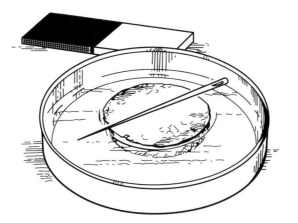

Wrong Readings

Does a Compass Always Give the Correct Direction?

Materials

compass

large piece of metal, like a belt buckle

Try This

1. Use the compass to position yourself so you are facing north.

2. Place the buckle near the compass. In which direction does the compass point?

What's Going On?

When you first read the compass, it gave you the accurate direction. When you held the compass near the buckle, the compass needle was attracted to the metal and gave an incorrect reading. Some rocks are magnetized, and even electrical power lines can influence a compass.

Magnet Strength

Which Is More Powerful, a Bar Magnet or a Horseshoe Magnet?

Materials

paper clips

bar magnet

horseshoe magnet (about the same size as the bar magnet)

Try This

1. Pick up as many paper clips as you can with the bar magnet.

2. Count the number of paper clips the magnet picked up.

3. Pick up as many paper clips as you can with the horseshoe magnet.

4. Count the number of paper clips the magnet picked up. Which magnet picked up more paper clips?

What's Going On?

The horseshoe magnet picked up more paper clips. The horseshoe magnet can pick up about three times as much weight as a bar magnet of the same size because its two poles are so close together that their attractive power is combined.

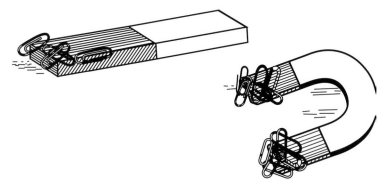

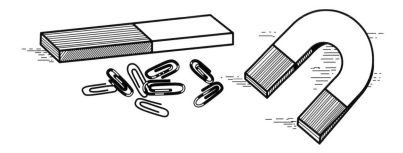

Magnet Chain

How Can Objects Become Temporarily Magnetized?

Materials

paper clips

bar magnet

Try This

1. Place a pile of paper clips on a table.

2. Dip the bar magnet into the pile and pick up as many paper clips as you can. How many paper clips are being held up that are not touching the magnet?

3. Remove all but one paper clip from the magnet.

4. Hold the one paper clip over another paper clip. What happens?

5. Continue this process until you have a line of paper clips.

6. Remove the first paper clip from the magnet. What happens to the rest of the paper clips?

What's Going On?

A magnetic force can be transferred through metals. This process enabled one paper clip to hold on to other paper clips as though it were a magnet. All the paper clips that touched the first paper clip became temporarily magnetized. When you removed the paper clip touching the magnet, all the other clips fell off.

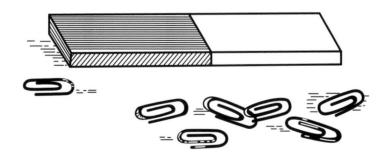

Magnetic Breakfast
What Can a Magnet Find in Cereal?

Materials

bar magnet

sealable plastic sandwich bag

iron-fortified cereal

bowl of water

piece of white paper

Try This

1. Crush a handful of iron-fortified cereal and put it in the bowl of water.

2. Place the bar magnet in the sealed plastic sandwich bag.

3. Dip the sealed magnet in the bowl and stir for several minutes.

4. Pull the bag out and hold it over the piece of paper.

5. Carefully pull the magnet up vertically out of the plastic bag.

What's Going On?

The small dark bits of material you see on the paper are iron. Humans need to eat some iron to be healthy. Iron is used by our blood cells to carry oxygen, for example. We usually get enough iron in our diet by eating iron-rich foods, such as dark, leafy vegetables, tofu, beans, and even dark chocolate. Some cereals and other processed foods have iron added to them.

Magnification

Magnification is the process of making objects appear larger than they really are. Objects can be made to look much larger or just a little larger through the use of differently shaped lenses. A **lens** is a curved transparent material that bends rays of light. Lenses are used in a variety of instruments, such as telescopes and microscopes. Magnification allows us to learn a great deal about our world. It lets us see the tiniest living creatures, as well as stars that are light-years away from Earth.

In this section, you will discover how Nature provides its own magnifying lens. You will also find out how eyeglasses, telescopes, and other magnifying devices work.

Water Magnifier
Where Did the Idea of Magnification Come From?

Materials

piece of wire

large nail

plastic cup

tap water

newspaper

Try This

1. Wrap the piece of wire around the nail to form a loop.

2. Slip the wire off the nail carefully to keep the shape you formed.

3. Dip the loop into a cup of tap water so a drop of water is trapped in the loop. Examine the drop of water in the loop.

4. Hold the loop over the newspaper and look through the water. What happens to the print?

What's Going On?

The newspaper print looked larger through the water magnifier. When you looked at the drop of water in the loop, you saw a bulge in the middle. Light waves get spread out by the curve of the water drop, enlarging whatever image the light waves carry. Water drops naturally magnify the things beneath them. Water drops may have given people the idea of making magnifiers.

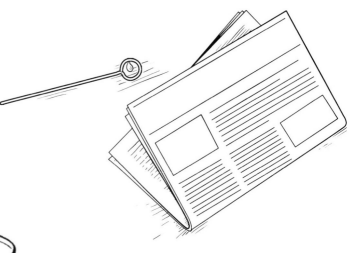

Comb Rays
How Does a Magnifying Lens Affect Light Rays?

Materials

4-in. (10-cm) circle cut out of cardboard

pencil

masking tape

comb

sheet of white paper

flashlight

magnifying lens

Try This

1. Poke a hole in the center of the cardboard circle with the pencil point and enlarge the hole with the pencil shaft.

2. Tape the comb over the hole.

3. Lay the sheet of white paper on a table.

4. Lay the flashlight next to the sheet. Position the cardboard circle between the flashlight and the sheet so the light shines through the hole.

5. Darken the room.

6. Hold the magnifying lens against the edge of the sheet so the light shines through it. What happens to the rays of light?

What's Going On?

Made of glass, the magnifying lens is a **double convex lens**, a lens that is thicker in the middle than around the edges. It bends the light rays, so they spread out, making an object look much larger when the light reaches your eyes.

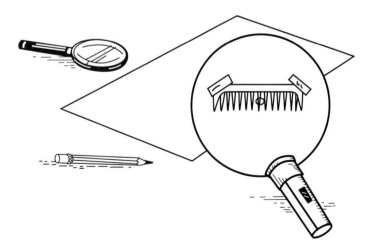

Magnifying Measurement

How Does the Distance of an Object from a Lens Affect the Object's Magnification?

Materials

sheet of graph paper

magnifying lens

pencil

Try This

1. Lay the sheet of graph paper on a table.

2. Place the magnifying lens over the sheet.

3. Count the number of squares you see through the magnifying lens. (You can mark them off with a pencil.)

4. Move the magnifying lens up higher, toward your eyes, and count the squares again. What are the results this time?

What's Going On?

The distance from a magnifying lens to an object determines the amount of magnification achieved or how large the object will look. As you increased the distance between the lens and the sheet of graph paper, you could see fewer squares, but they were larger.

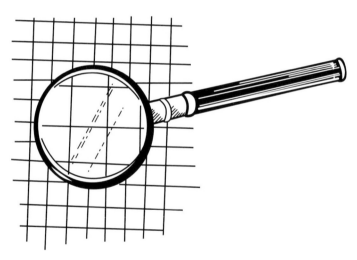

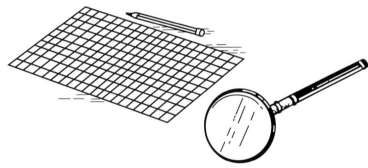

Double Convex

How Does a Double Convex Lens Work?

Materials

magnifying lens

sheet of white paper

Try This

1. Darken all the windows in the room except the one at which you are working.
2. Hold the magnifying lens in your right hand.
3. Position the lens so it focuses on an object outside.
4. Hold the sheet of white paper in your left hand.
5. Move the paper slowly toward the lens until you see the outside object on the paper. What do you notice about the image?

What's Going On?

The image on the sheet of paper was upside down. The magnifying lens is thicker in the middle than at the edges. This double convex lens caused the light rays that were approaching from different directions to meet at one point called the **focal point**. The light rays then continued past the focal point and crossed each other. By the time the light rays reached the paper, they were reversed. The rays that came from the bottom of the object were at the top, and those that came from the top of the object were at the bottom. To see an object right-side up through a magnifying lens, the object you are looking at must be closer to the lens than the focal point.

Word Flip

How Can You Make Words Turn Upside Down?

Materials

book

2 magnifying lenses

Try This

1. Open the book and lay it on a table.

2. Place one magnifying lens on top of the other on the book.

3. Look through both lenses at the words on the page.

4. Slowly move the lenses toward you. What do you see?

What's Going On?

The two magnifying lenses made the words look slightly larger when they were close to the book. As you moved the lenses away from the book, the words appeared much larger. When you moved the lenses still farther away, the words suddenly turned upside down. This happened because light rays bent by the lens crossed over each other beyond the focal point.

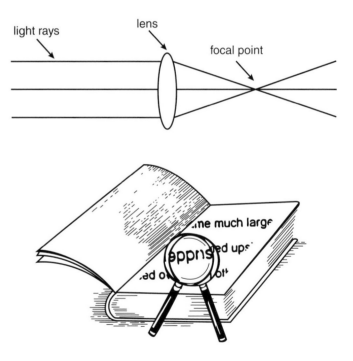

Round Works

Why Must a Magnifying Lens Always Be Round?

Materials

tap water

round glass

square glass

2 drinking straws

Try This

1. Pour tap water into the round and square glasses three-fourths of the way up.

2. Place a drinking straw in each glass.

3. Look at the straws to see if they are both magnified.

What's Going On?

When you looked at the round glass, you saw that the straw was magnified. The square glass did not magnify the straw. The curve of the glass acted as a magnifying lens. The light that bent toward the thickest part of the magnifying lens came to a point. The square glass is the same thickness throughout, so it did not cause light to magnify.

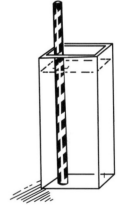

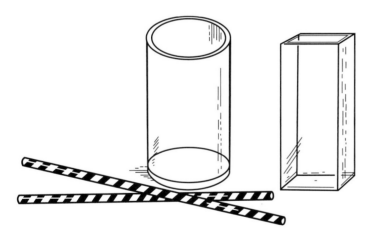

Shadow Look
How Does a Magnifying Lens Affect Shadows?

Materials

piece of white cardboard

plastic cup

ruler

flashlight

magnifying lens

Try This

1. Place the piece of cardboard on the floor so it is leaning against a wall.

2. Place the plastic cup on the floor about 8 in. (20 cm) in front of the cardboard.

3. Direct the flashlight beam on the cup and look at the shadow cast on the cardboard.

4. Place the magnifying lens between the cup and the cardboard.

5. Again, direct the flashlight beam on the cup.

6. Move the flashlight back and forth to get a clear shadow. Is the shadow larger or smaller than the shadow that was cast without the magnifying lens?

What's Going On?

The shadow cast by the cup was smaller when the magnifying lens was placed between the cup and the cardboard. A shadow is the absence of direct light rays. When you placed the magnifying lens in front of the cup, it picked up the rays coming around the outside of the cup and bent them inward. Because the magnifier channeled this light to the cardboard, the cup's shadow was smaller.

Eyeglass Lenses
How Do Eyeglasses Help People See Better?

Materials

one or more pairs of prescription eyeglasses, borrowed from friends

Try This

1. Try on one of the pairs of eyeglasses.

2. Look at a faraway object and a close-up object. How do your eyes focus on these objects?

3. Follow the same procedure with the other pairs of glasses.

What's Going On

Each type of lens helps correct a specific eyesight problem. Concave lenses are used for **nearsighted** people, who can clearly see objects close to them, but distant objects are blurred. This type of corrective lens is thinner in the middle than around the edges – it bends light rays outward before they reach the eye, so the rays focus on the retina instead of in front of it. A **farsighted** person can focus well on objects at a distance, but close-up objects are blurred. These people must wear glasses with convex lenses – lenses that are thicker in the middle than around the edges. Convex lenses bend the light rays inward, so they focus on the retina instead of behind it.

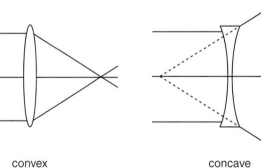

convex   concave

Telescope Image
How Does a Telescope Work?

Materials

hand mirror

pocket mirror

magnifying lens

to be performed on a moonlit night

Try This

1. Lay the hand mirror on a flat surface by a window facing the Moon.

2. Hold the pocket mirror in one hand so you can see a reflection of the hand mirror in the middle of it.

3. Hold the magnifying lens in the other hand so you can see the reflection of the Moon in the pocket mirror. First look at the reflection of the Moon in the pocket mirror, and then look at the Moon directly.

What's Going On?

The Moon looked much nearer when you looked through the magnifying lens at the Moon's reflection in the pocket mirror than when you looked directly at the Moon. A **telescope** uses lenses and mirrors to collect and enlarge images of faraway objects. In this simple model, the magnifying lens enlarged the image in the mirror but did not collect additional light. To collect additional light, a second, bigger lens would have to replace the pocket mirror.

Image by Free-Photos from Pixabay

Water

Water is a clear, colorless liquid that covers most of the Earth's surface. It is essential to every person, animal, and plant. In fact, more than half your body is made up of water!

Water has many interesting properties, which you will learn about in this section. You will discover how you can make water come out of air, what makes objects float, and why water is good for taking showers in.

Sticky Water

Can You Pick Stuff Up with Water?

Materials

piece of tape

eye dropper

small container of water

plate

black pepper flakes

Try This

1. Pour a pinch of pepper on the plate.

2. See if you can pick up some of the pepper using the tape.

3. Fill the eye dropper with water.

4. Push a single drop of water out the end of the eye dropper. Keep it attached to the end of the eye dropper.

5. See if you can pick up any pepper flakes using the drop of water at the end of the eye dropper.

What's Going On?

We don't usually think of water as sticky, but it is. The pepper stuck to the water just like it stuck to the tape. When water has nothing else to stick to, it sticks to itself. That's why raindrops are mostly round. If water wasn't sticky at all, you would have trouble getting your toothbrush wet to brush your teeth, and taking a shower wouldn't work, because you'd stay dry the whole time.

Water Skin

Why Does Water Form a Surface?

Materials

plate

penny

eye dropper

tap water

small container or bowl

Try This

1. Place the penny on the plate.

2. Fill the container with tap water.

3. Using the eye dropper, add a drop of water at a time to the top of the penny, trying to keep the water from spilling over the sides of the penny.

4. When the water has filled the top of the penny, look closely at the water on the penny from the side and top. Notice the water at the penny's edge. See how many more drops of water you can gently add before the water spills over the side.

What's Going On?

When you looked at the penny from the side, you noticed a bulge over the top of the water. The water came up over the rim of the penny but did not spill over the sides. The force holding the water in place is known as **surface tension**. Water molecules are attracted to one another and tend to hold together, even more so at the surface, so that there is a thin, invisible "skin" on top of the surface of water. Some insects are able to walk on water because they use the water's surface tension for support.

Circle Thread
How Can You Change Surface Tension?

Materials

piece of cotton thread

plastic cup

tap water

dishwashing liquid

Try This

1. Tie the ends of the piece of cotton thread to form a loop.

2. Fill the plastic cup with tap water.

3. Wet the thread and place it on the water in the cup. What shape does it form?

4. Put one drop of the dishwashing liquid inside the loop. What happens to the loop now?

What's Going On?

When you put the loop of thread into the water, it formed an irregular shape. When you added the dishwashing liquid, the thread moved out to form a perfect circle. The surface tension of the water is equal across the surface of the water. Dishwashing liquid makes it hard for water molecules to hold on to one another. When you put the dishwashing liquid into the water, the surface tension inside the thread was weakened, so the tension outside the loop was greater than that inside. Like a little tear in a piece of fabric, the water's surface tension outside the loop pulled the water surface inside the loop apart.

Water Vapor

What Causes Water to Collect on the Outside of a Cold Glass?

Materials

clean, dry glass

timer

You must have access to a freezer.

Try This

1. Place the glass in the freezer for 2 minutes.

2. Remove the glass from the freezer and wait 1 minute. What do you see on the sides of the glass?

What's Going On?

There is almost always water vapor in the air. Water vapor is water in gas form. Water vapor is mixed in with all the other molecules that make up the air. When you removed the glass from the freezer, warm water vapor from the air hit the sides of the cool glass. When the warm vapor cooled, it turned back into a liquid. The same process happens at night when dew forms on grass.

Window Fog

Does Your Breath Contain Water?

Materials

a window on a cold day

Try This

1. Place your face close to the window.

2. Exhale on the window.
   What happens?

What's Going On?

You created a fog on the window. When you exhaled, you gave off water vapor that you cannot generally see. Water condenses into a liquid when it hits a cold surface.

Water vapor doesn't just come out of our mouths; it actually comes out of our skin all the time. That's one reason why you must drink lots of water.

Breathing Dirt
Does Water Ever Fall Up?

Materials

a small piece of plastic, about the size of a placemat or larger

Try This

1. Place the plastic on the grass on a warm day.
2. Come back in 10 minutes and feel the bottom of the plastic.

What's Going On?

When you felt the underside of the plastic, it was probably a little damp. Soil contains a lot of water. Even though you cannot see it, this water is slowly rising into the air as water vapor all the time. When enough water vapor rises high up where the air gets colder, clouds form.

Sinking Ship
How Does a Boat Float?

Materials

2 same-sized sheets of aluminum foil

tap water

2 plastic bowls

spoon

Try This

1. Fill a bowl with water.

2. Press the rounded part of the spoon into the top of the water and then lift the spoon up again. Try this a few times and observe what happens each time to the surface of the water where the spoon presses in.

3. Form one sheet of the aluminum foil into the shape of a boat that has sides.

4. Crumple the other sheet into a ball.

5. Pour tap water into the other plastic bowl.

6. Place one piece of foil in each bowl.

What's Going On?

The boat-shaped sheet of foil floated, but the ball-shaped sheet sank. Why? An object will float if the amount of water that is **displaced** (pushed out of the way) weighs the same as the object. This is because the water pushed out of the way of the boat tries to return to the area it was pushed out of. You could see this each time you pressed the spoon into the surface of the water: when you removed the spoon, there was no dent in the water, because the water is always rushing back in to create a flat surface. An object will sink if the displaced water weighs less than the object. In that case, there isn't enough water trying to rush back in to keep the object up at the surface. The object's shape will affect how much water is displaced. The wide flat bottom of a boat displaces a lot of water.

Leakproof

Can You Puncture a Bag of Water and Have Nothing Leak Out?

Materials

zip tight sealable gallon-sized plastic bag

several freshly sharpened pencils

tap water

Try This

1. Fill the bag with water.

2. Hold the bag over a sink.

3. Without hesitation, drive a sharpened pencil straight through the wall of the bag. Drive the pencil out the other side.

4. See how many pencils you can drive through the bag.

What's Going On?

The bag is made of long sticky molecules, almost like invisible cooked spaghetti. When you drive a pencil through the bag, the long molecules part around the pencil. The pressure of the water trying to escape presses the bag's long molecules back up against the pencil quickly, stopping the water from getting out.

Level Look

Why Does Water Form a Level Surface?

Materials

plastic funnel

clear plastic tubing (that fits on the end of the funnel)

tap water

food coloring

helper

Try This

1. Fit the plastic funnel into one end of the plastic tubing.

2. Holding up both ends of the tubing, ask your helper to pour tap water into the tubing through the funnel until the tubing is about half full.

3. Ask your helper to add one drop of food coloring. Then shake the tubing.

4. Remove the funnel from the tubing and hold the ends of the tubing in different positions, with one end higher than the other. Notice the water level in each half of the tubing.

5. Continue experimenting with the positions of the ends of the tubing as you watch the water levels.

What's Going On?

When you held one end of the tubing higher on one side, the water in the other side of the tubing shifted, so that the water level was always the same on both sides. The water level on one side never rose above that on the other side. The downward weight of the air on one side of the tube is the same as the weight of air on the other side of the tube, so the water keeps adjusting as you move the tube. **Altitude** is the height of land above sea level. It is measured starting at sea level all around the world because, just like in the tube, the ocean is generally at the same level everywhere on the planet.

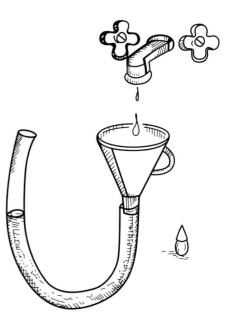

Image by David Mark from Pixabay

Weather

Rain, wind, sunshine, snow, thunder, lightning, floods, and tornados – weather is a beautiful, exciting, and sometimes dangerous part of our world. Weather is the condition of the Earth's atmosphere at a particular time and place. Many different factors make up weather. Some conditions of the atmosphere that can be measured are temperature, air pressure, wind speed, and moisture.

In this section, you will learn more about weather, the objects that help predict weather, and the effects of weather. You will learn how the location of thermometers affects their readings. You will create lightning. And you will even use a cricket as a weather forecaster.

Wind Sail

How Does the Sun Affect Air?

Materials

lamp without a shade with an incandescent light bulb

timer

baby powder

Try This

1. Turn on the lamp for about 5 minutes. *Caution: Do not touch the light bulb; it may get very hot.*

2. Sprinkle a tiny pinch of the baby powder above the light bulb. What happens?

What's Going On?

The powder floated upward. When the light bulb warmed up, it also warmed the air above it. Warm air rises, because it becomes lighter than colder air. Every day, the Sun warms the Earth and heats the air above it. Cool air moves down to take the place of warm air. This movement of warm and cool air masses is what causes most winds.

Wind Direction

How Can You Instantly Tell Which Direction the Wind Is Coming From?

Materials

your finger on a windy day

Try This

1. Wet your finger.
2. Hold your finger in the wind. What do you feel?

What's Going On?

One side of your finger felt cooler than the other side. The cooler side was the side that faced the wind. The wind caused the liquid on one side of your finger to evaporate quickly, making your finger feel cool. This is how sweat works to cool us down too.

Wind Wheel

How Can You Tell How Fast the Wind Is Blowing?

Materials

pencil

paper plate

different-colored marking pens

4 small paper cups

stapler

long, thin nail

button

hammer

wooden stake

adult helper

Try This

1. With the pencil, mark off four equal sections on the paper plate.

2. With the marking pens, color each section a different color.

3. Place one paper cup on its side in each colored section ½ in. (1.25 cm) from the edge of the plate so the cups face counterclockwise.

4. Staple the cups to the plate.

5. With the nail, punch a hole through the middle of the plate.

6. Push the nail through a buttonhole and then through the plate.

7. Ask your adult helper to hammer the nail into a wooden stake so the plate faces the direction from which you think the wind is blowing the hardest. Wait for the wind to blow and watch your wind wheel.

What's Going On?

You created a simple **anemometer**, an instrument that measures wind speed. The wind pushed all the cups in the same direction, making the wheel turn. By observing how quickly the different colors blend together, you can see about how fast the wind is blowing.

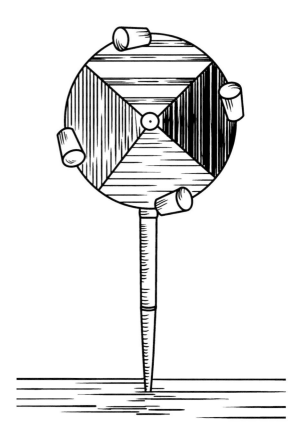

Wind Chill

How Does Wind Affect Temperature?

Materials

2 thermometers

container of tap water

piece of absorbent cloth

perform on a cool, windy day

Try This

1. Find the temperature outdoors

2. Fill a container with water, using the hot and cold taps to make the water as close to the air temperature outside as possible.

3. Take both thermometers outside, with the container of water and absorbent cloth, and set them near each other.

4. Wrap one end of the piece of cloth around the bulb of one thermometer.

5. Place the other end of the cloth in the bowl of water.

6. Return in about 10 minutes and record the temperature on each thermometer.

What's Going On?

How hot or cold the day feels isn't just about what the thermometer reads; it's also about how much the air is moving. When the air moves, it removes heated moisture from the surface of our skin. On cool, windy days, that means it actually feels much colder than the thermometer reading. The term **wind chill** was developed to account for the cooling effects of the wind on your skin. The stronger the wind, the lower the temperature adjusted for wind chill will be. The wet thermometer gives a better approximation of the temperature we feel, because, as the wind blows, the moisture evaporates from the cloth, taking away some of the heat from the air around the bulb.

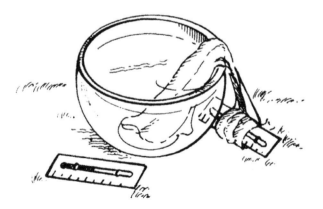

When you are checking the temperature outside to decide what to wear, what really matters is the wind chill temperature. For example, if the actual temperature outside is 25 °F (14 °C), but the wind is blowing at 20 mi (32 km) an hour, the temperature will feel as though it is about −3 °F (−20 °C). Thick coat, hat, and gloves for sure!

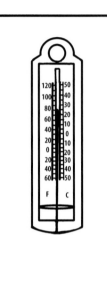

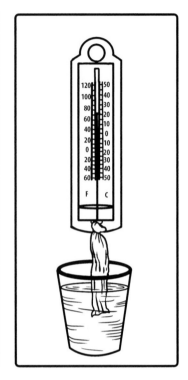

Dew Point

When Will Dew Form on the Grass?

Materials

thermometer

empty tin can with label removed

warm tap water

ice cubes

spoon

Try This

1. Note the air temperature outside the tin can.

2. Pour warm tap water into the can about three-fourths of the way up.

3. Place the thermometer in the can.

4. Add a few ice cubes, one at a time, and stir with the spoon.

5. Keep adding cubes and stirring until a mist forms on the outside of the can. *Note: Do not use the thermometer to stir.*

6. Read the temperature on the thermometer when the mist just begins to form.

What's Going On?

The temperature you read is the **dew point**, the temperature at which water vapor forms droplets. As the temperature inside the can dropped, the water vapor touching the cold can also became cooler. This water vapor turned into liquid, called **dew**, and stuck to the can.

At the same time, the air was taking away (evaporating) the water on the outside of the can. At the dew point, evaporation was no longer taking place faster than the rate at which the water was sticking to the can, so the can stayed wet.

The amount of water vapor in the air determines the temperature at which water vapor forms on the side of the can. It also tells you the temperature at which dew will form on grass. At night, when temperatures drop, the air can't hold as much water vapor, and it starts to settle as dew.

Create Lightning
Where Does Lightning Come From?

Materials

two balloons

wool cloth

Try This

1. Inflate both balloons.

2. Rub one balloon on the wool (or on your hair) for about a minute in one direction and the other against a smooth wall.

3. Darken the room.

4. Hold a balloon in each hand and slowly move the balloons close together. What happens?

What's Going On?

Every object is made up of many smaller particles. Rubbing the balloons on the cloth and on the wall changed how many particles of certain types were on the surface of the balloons. The particles like to be in balance, so when you held the balloons close to each other, some particles jumped from one to the other. This stream of particles is a kind of electricity called **static electricity**. Lightning is a giant example of static electricity, where particles jump from clouds to the ground. The movement of air causes friction and can cause particles to pile up at the bottom of a cloud. When the difference between the clouds and ground is large enough, lightning flashes to balance things out.

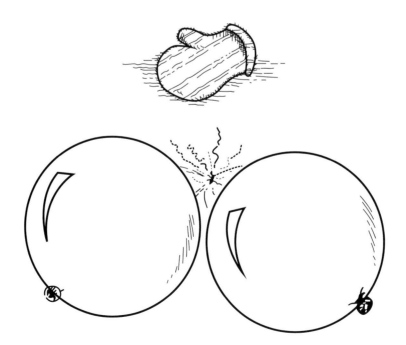

Thunder Wonder

Why Does Thunder Arrive After Lightning?

Materials

tape measure (the longer the better)

a large outdoor space

a basketball

Try This

1. Measure out a distance outdoors of 500 ft.

2. Stand at one end of this length, while a friend stands at the other.

3. Have your friend clap their hands or bounce the basketball on the ground.

What's Going On?

You saw your friend clap or the ball hit the ground before you heard this. This is because light travels faster than sound. Light travels about one million times faster than sound. This is why, when lightning strikes, the light from the bolt reaches your eyes before the rumble of thunder reaches your ears. In half a second, the sound of thunder travels about 500 ft. In the same amount of time, the light of lightning travels about 500 million ft (about 95 000 mi, or half the distance between the Earth and the Moon). You can use this to figure out how far away a lightning strike was. Since sound travels about 1000 ft in a second, and a mile is roughly 5000 ft long, after 5 seconds sound has traveled about a mile. To use this, start counting seconds after you see lightning. When you hear the thunder, stop counting. Divide that number by 5. The answer is the number of miles away the lightning struck.

No Pressure

How Does a Barometer Help Predict the Weather?

Materials

plastic bowl

tap water

2-liter soda bottle

ruler

marker

Try This

1. Draw short lines along the length of the bottle, every inch or couple centimeters, and number them.

2. Half fill the plastic bowl with tap water.

3. Pour water into the soda bottle three-fourths of the way up.

4. Place your hand over the mouth of the bottle and turn the bottle upside down.

5. Place the mouth of the upside-down bottle on the bottom of the bowl. Remove your hand carefully and quickly.

What's Going On?

This simple **barometer** can help you predict the weather. The air pressure inside the bottle stays the same. The changing pressure of the outside air on the water in the bowl causes the water level inside the bottle to rise and fall. Rising air pressure pushes water up into the bottle. Falling air pressure causes the water level in the bottle to drop. High pressure usually means better weather, as clouds are pushed out of an area, whereas low pressure indicates colder temperatures or rain.

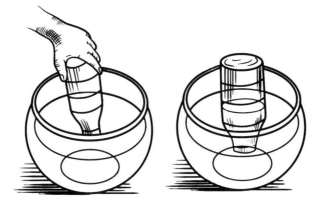

Cricket Thermometer

How Can Animals Forecast Weather Conditions?

Materials

crickets

watch or timer with seconds

thermometer

Try This

1. Find a rural or suburban area where you can listen to crickets in the evening.

2. Using the second hand on the watch, count the number of chirps a cricket makes in 15 seconds.

3. Add 40 to the number of chirps you counted to get a temperature in degrees Fahrenheit. (To determine what the cricket in your area can tell you about the temperature, you may need to use the centigrade scale. In that case, use this simple method: Subtract 32 from the number of chirps you counted, multiply by 5, and divide by 9.)

4. Compare this number to the actual temperature outside by using a thermometer.

What's Going On?

Since temperature affects the movement of things, it influences all creatures. Everything creatures do requires chemical reactions to happen inside their bodies. The speed of chemical reactions that happen inside a cricket is directly impacted by the temperature around them. On warm days, crickets chirp more quickly; on cold days, crickets chirp more slowly.

The math might be a little different where you are, for the crickets in your area. How can you improve the equation to get a better measurement?

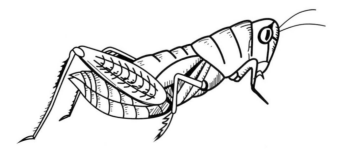

Glossary

abdomen   rear part of an insect's body

absorb   take something in

adductor   strong muscle of an oyster that attaches the oyster's body to its shell

amplifier   device that makes sounds louder

anemometer   instrument used to measure wind speed

antennae   delicate, long pair of movable parts on the top of an insect's head used for smelling and touching

atom   smallest part of a material that retains the properties of that material

attract   pull toward

ballast tanks   air and water tanks that make a submarine move up and down in the water

barometer   any instrument used to measure atmospheric pressure

biceps   large set of muscles in the upper arm

carbon dioxide   gas made up of carbon and oxygen

cartilage   soft, bonelike material between bones

center of gravity   point at which the whole of an object's weight is concentrated

chromatography   technique for separating chemical substances by taking advantage of the different rates at which the substances are absorbed from a moving liquid

chromosomes   tiny parts of a cell that carry genes

colors   sensations produced by visible light entering the human eye

compass   instrument used for determining directions

concave   having a hollowed surface; bending inward

concentrated   full strength; not mixed with anything

condensation   change of the state of a substance from a vapor to a liquid

cones   special parts of the eye that distinguish colors

converted   changed

convex   having a protruding surface; bending outward

deflate   collapse by letting out air

density   a measure of weight in relation to volume

dew   warm, moist air that comes into contact with cooler objects, causing moisture to appear on them

dew point   temperature on a thermometer when dew or vapor just begins to form

diameter   distance across the middle of a circle

dilute   make weaker

displaced   pushed out of the way

double convex lens   a lens that is thicker in the middle than at the edges

dye   coloring substance

elastic   material that returns to its original state after it has been distorted by a force

electromagnet   temporary magnet that allows the flow of electricity through a wire

energy   ability to do work

farsighted   able to see distant objects better than close-up objects

focal point   point at which lines of light come together

force   power or energy that creates something

friction   the force that resists motion between two objects rubbing against one another

fulcrum   point at which a lever rests when lifting an object

gears   wheels with teeth around the edges that come together and turn each other

gene   small unit of a cell that passes characteristics from one generation to another

genetics   the study of why living things look and behave as they do

gravity   force that attracts objects to the center of the Earth and keeps planets and other heavenly bodies in orbit

hemisphere   half section of the Earth

humidity   amount of water vapor in the air

ignite   set on fire

inflate   put air into an object so that it expands

iris   colored part of the eye around the pupil

kaleidoscope small tube of mirrors in which patterns are produced

kinetic energy energy due to motion

latex elastic type of material

left valve the part of an oyster that attaches to objects in the water

lens curved transparent material that bends rays of light

lever bar resting on a support that is pushed down at one end to lift the other end

light form of energy that is the source of illumination

lightning flash in the sky produced when electricity passes from one cloud to another

lines of force lines in the field around a magnet that show which poles attract and which repel

liquid matter in a state in which molecules are able to move around but are still held in contact with the molecules around them

machine any device that modifies a force so work can be done more easily

magnet a material that attracts certain other materials, such as metals

magnetic having the properties of magnets

magnetic field the attraction area around magnets

mantle fold of tissue lining an oyster's shell

metabolism process in living things that turns food into energy, new cells, and waste

mirror a surface that reflects most of the light falling on it

molecule smallest part of an element or compound capable of leading a separate existence

mollusk animal that grows a shell to protect itself

nearsighted able to see close-up objects better than distant objects

organism living thing

ovipositor long, pointed, divided segment of an insect's body at the end of the abdomen used for laying eggs in soft ground

particles very tiny pieces

pendulum   weight hanging from a fixed point

periscope   instrument that makes it possible to see around corners

pigment   substance in things that gives color

pivot   point at which something turns

plastron   under-shell of a turtle

plumb line   device used to find vertical lines

poles   north and south ends of a magnet

polluted   unclean, impure, or dirty

potential energy   energy that is stored

pressure   force acting on each unit of area of a surface

primary colors   yellow, blue, and red

pulley   simple machine using rope and one or more wheels to change the direction of a force

pulse   regular beating in the arteries caused by movements of the heart as it pumps blood

pupil   opening in the center of the eye

rainbow   arc-shaped band of colors

reflect   bounce light off

refract   bend light

repel   push away

resistance   ability to with-stand a force

secondary colors   combina-tions of two primary colors

secrete   give off or release

segment   section

shadow   the dark area where light rays would have fallen if not for an object in the way

solar energy   energy from the sun

spectrum   a series of col-ored bands of light that can be seen when light is broken up, such as by a prism

spinal column   long row of connected bones forming the backbone

spinal cord   nerve tissue running down the spinal column

static electricity   stationary electric charge

stethoscope   instrument for listening to sounds of the body

surface tension force that attracts water molecules to one another and that holds the surface of water together

telescope optical device containing lenses and mirrors for magnifying distant objects

thermometer device for measuring temperature

thorax middle part of an insect's body

triceps small set of muscles in the upper arm

vapor a substance in its gas state

vertebrates animals with a backbone

vertical straight up and down

viscosity ability of fluids to flow

volume amount of space inside something

weight downward force exerted on an object by gravity

wind chill cooling effects of the winds and temperatures on skin

Further Reading

Cash, Terry. *101 Physics Tricks* (New York: Sterling Publishing, 1991).

Frank, Marjorie. *202 Science Investigations* (Nashville, TN: Incentive Publications, 1990).

Glover, David. *Batteries, Bulbs and Wires* (New York: Kingfisher Books, 1993a).

Glover, David. *Flying and Floating* (New York: Kingfisher Books, 1993b).

Glover, David. *Solids and Liquids* (New York: Kingfisher Books, 1993c).

Grafton, Allison, and Levine, Shari. *Projects for a Healthy Planet* (New York Wiley, 1992).

Hann, Judith. *How Science Works*, (Pleasantville, NY: Reader's Digest Association, 1991).

Headlam, Catherine. *Kingfisher Science Encyclopedia* (New York: Kingfisher Books, 1991).

Herbert, Don. *Mr. Wizard's Supermarket Science* (New York: Random House, 1980).

Kendra, Margaret, and Williams, Phyllis S. *Science Wizardry for Kids* (Hauppauge, NY: Barron's Educational Series, 1992).

Kerrod, Robin. *How Things Work* (New York: Marshall Cavendish, 1990).

Kohl, MaryAnn, and Potter, Jean. *ScienceArts* (Bellingham, WA: Bright Ring Publishing, 1993).

Lewis, James. *Hocus Pocus Stir and Cook: The Kitchen Science Magic Book* (New York: Meadowbrook Press, 1991).

Lorbiecki, Marybeth, and Mowery, Linda. *Earthwise at Home* (Minneapolis, MN: Carolrhoda Books).

Mandell, Muriel. *Simple Science Experiments with Everyday Materials* (New York: Sterling Publishing, 1989).

Orii, Eiji, and Orii, Masako. *Light* (Milwaukee, WI: Gareth Stevens Publishing, 1989).

Simon, Seymour. *Mirror Magic* (Honesdale, PA: Boyds Mills Press, 1980).

Smithsonian Institution. *Color and Light* (Milwaukee, WI: Gareth Stevens Publishing, 1993).

Stier, Sam. *Engineering Education for the Next Generation:* A Nature-Inspired Approach (W.W. Norton & Co., 2020).

Taylor, Barbara. *Green Thumbs Up: The Science of Growing Plants* (New York: Random House, 1991).

Taylor, Kim. *Structure* (New York: Wiley, 1992).

VanCleave, Janice. *Janice VanCleave's Biology for Every Kid* (New York: Wiley, 1993a).

VanCleave, Janice. *Janice VanCleave's Earth Science for Every Kid* (New York: Wiley, 1993b).

VanCleave, Janice. *Janice VanCleave's Microscopes and Magnifying Lenses* (New York: Wiley, 1993c).

Watt, Fiona. *Planet Earth* (Tulsa, OK: EDC Publishing, 1991).

Williams, John. *Air* (Milwaukee, WI: Gareth Stevens Publishing, 1992a).

Williams, John. *Water* (Milwaukee, WI: Gareth Stevens Publishing, 1992b).

Williams, John. *Color and Light*, (Milwaukee, WI: Gareth Stevens Publishing, 1993).

Index